ISBN 978-1-331-74925-7
PIBN 10229767

English
Français
Deutsche
Italiano
Español
Português

www.forgottenbooks.com

Mythology Photography **Fiction**
Fishing Christianity **Art** Cooking
Essays Buddhism Freemasonry
Medicine **Biology** Music **Ancient
Egypt** Evolution Carpentry Physics
Dance Geology **Mathematics** Fitness
Shakespeare **Folklore** Yoga Marketing
Confidence Immortality Biographies
Poetry **Psychology** Witchcraft
Electronics Chemistry History **Law**
Accounting **Philosophy** Anthropology
Alchemy Drama Quantum Mechanics
Atheism Sexual Health **Ancient History**
Entrepreneurship Languages Sport
Paleontology Needlework Islam
Metaphysics Investment Archaeology
Parenting Statistics Criminology
Motivational

JOHN DENHAM PARSONS

LONDON

SIMPKIN, MARSHALL HAMILTON KENT & CO., LIMITED

1896

Printed by Bemrose & Sons, Ltd., Derby and London.

"O CRUX, SPLENDIDIOR CUNCTIS ASTRIS, MUNDO CELEBRIS, HOMINIBUS MULTUM AMABILIS, SANCTIOR UNIVERSIS."

[*BREVIARIUM ROMANUM,*

Festival of the Invention of the Holy Cross.]

PREFACE.

THE history of the symbol of the cross has had an attraction for the author ever since, as an enquiring youth, he found himself unable to obtain satisfactory answers to four questions concerning the same which presented themselves to his mind.

The first of those questions was why John the Baptist, who was beheaded before Jesus was executed, and so far as we are told never had anything to do with a cross, is represented in our religious pictures as holding a cross.

The second question was whether this curious but perhaps in itself easily explained practice, had in its inception any connection with the non-Mosaic initiatory rite of baptism ; which Jesus accepted as a matter of course at the hands of his cousin John, and in which the sign of the cross has for ages been the all-important feature. And it was the wonder whether there was or was not some association between the facts that the New Testament writers give no explanation whatever of the origin of baptism as an initiatory rite, that this non-Mosaic initiatory rite was in use among Sun-God worshippers long before our era, and that the Fathers admitted that the followers of the Persian conception of the Sun-God marked their initiates upon the forehead like the followers of the Christ, which finally induced the author to start a systematic enquiry into the history of the cross as a symbol.

The third question was why, despite the fact that the instrument of execution to which

Jesus was affixed can have had but one shape, almost any kind of cross is accepted as a symbol of our faith.

The last of the four questions was why many varieties of the cross of four equal arms, which certainly was not a representation of an instrument of execution, were accepted by Christians as symbols of the Christ before any cross which could possibly have been a representation of an instrument of execution was given a place among the symbols of Christianity; while even nowadays one variety of the cross of four equal arms is the favourite symbol of the Greek Church, and both it and the other varieties enter into the ornamentation of our sacred properties and dispute the supremacy with the cross which has one of its arms longer than the other three.

Pursuing these matters for himself, the author eventually found that even before our era the cross was venerated by many as the symbol of Life ; though our works of reference seldom mention this fact, and never do it justice.

He moreover discovered that no one has ever written a complete history of the symbol, showing the possibility that the *stauros* or post to which Jesus was affixed was not cross-shaped, and the certainty that, in any case, what eventually became the symbol of our faith owed some of its prestige as a Christian symbol of Victory and Life to the position it occupied in pre-Christian days.

The author has therefore, in the hope of drawing attention to the subject, incorporated the results of his researches in the present essay.

14, St. Dunstan's Hill,
    London, E.C.

CONTENTS

THE NON-CHRISTIAN CROSS.

CHAPTER I.

WAS THE *STAUROS* OF JESUS CROSS-SHAPED?

IN the thousand and one works supplied for our information upon matters connected with the history of our race, we are told that Alexander the Great, Titus, and various Greek, Roman, and Oriental rulers of ancient days, "crucified" this or that person ; or that they "crucified" so many at once, or during their reign. And the instrument of execution is called a "cross."

The natural result is that we imagine that all the people said to have been "crucified" were executed by being nailed or otherwise affixed to a cross-shaped instrument set in the ground, like that to be seen in our fanciful illustrations of the execution of Jesus.

This was, however, by no means necessarily the case.

For instance, the death spoken of, death by the *stauros*, included transfixion by a pointed stauros or stake, as well as affixion to an un-pointed stauros or stake ; and the latter punishment was not always that referred to.

It is also probable that in most of the many cases where we have no clue as to which kind of stauros was used, the cause of the condemned one's death was transfixion by a pointed stauros.

Moreover, even if we could prove that this very common mode of capital punishment was in no case that referred to by the historians who lived in bygone ages, and that death was in each instance caused by affixion to, instead of transfixion by, a stauros, we should still have to prove that each stauros had a cross-bar before we could correctly describe the death caused by it as death by crucifixion.

It is also, upon the face of it, somewhat un-likely that the ancients would in every instance in which they despatched a man by affixing him to a post set in the ground, have gone out of their way to provide the artistic but quite unnecessary cross-bar of our imaginations.

As it is, in any case, well known that the Romans very often despatched those condemned to death by affixing them to a stake or post which had no cross-bar, the question arises as to what proof we have that a cross-bar was used in the case of Jesus.

Nor is the question an unimportant one. For, as we shall see in the chapters to come, there was a pre-Christian cross, which was, like ours, a symbol of Life. And it must be obvious to all that if the cross was a symbol of Life before our era, it is possible that it was originally fixed upon as a symbol of the Christ because it was a symbol of Life ; the assumption that it became a symbol of Life because it was a symbol of the Christ, being in that case neither more nor less than a very natural instance of putting the cart before the horse.

Now the Greek word which in Latin versions of the New Testament is translated as *crux*, and in English versions is rendered as *cross*, *i.e.*, the word *stauros*, seems to have, at the beginning of our era, no more meant a cross than the English word stick means a crutch.

It is true that a stick may be in the shape of a crutch, and that the stauros to which Jesus was affixed may have been in the shape of a cross. But just as the former is not necessarily a crutch, so the latter was not necessarily a cross.

What the ancients used to signify when they used the word *stauros*, can easily be seen by referring to either the Iliad or the Odyssey.[1]

It will there be found to clearly signify an ordinary pole or stake without any cross-bar. And it is as thus signifying a single piece of wood that the word in question is used throughout the old Greek classics.[2]

The stauros used as an instrument of execution was (1) a small pointed pole or stake used for thrusting through the body, so as to pin the latter to the earth, or otherwise render death inevitable; (2) a similar pole or stake fixed in the ground point upwards, upon which the condemned one was forced down till incapable of escaping; (3) a much longer and stouter pole or stake fixed point upwards, upon which the victim, with his hands tied behind him, was lodged in such a way that the point should enter his breast and the weight of the

---

[1] *e.g., Iliad,* xxiv. 453 ; *Odyssey,* xiv. 11.
[2] *e.g.,* Thuc. iv. 90 ; Xen. *An.* v. 2, 21.

body cause every movement to hasten the end ; and (4) a stout unpointed pole or stake set upright in the earth, from which the victim was suspended by a rope round his wrists, which were first tied behind him so that the position might become an agonising one ; or to which the doomed one was bound, or, as in the case of Jesus, nailed.

That this last named kind of stauros, which was admittedly that to which Jesus was affixed, had in every case a cross-bar attached, is untrue ; that it had in most cases, is unlikely ; that it had in the case of Jesus, is unproven.

Even as late as the Middle Ages, the word stauros seems to have primarily signified a straight piece of wood without a cross-bar. For the famous Greek lexicographer, Suidas, expressly states, " Stauroi ; ortha xula perpé-gota," and both Eustathius and Hesychius affirm that it meant a *straight* stake or pole.

The side light thrown upon the question by Lucian is also worth noting. This writer, referring to Jesus, alludes to " That sophist of theirs who was fastened to a *skolops ;* " which word signified a single piece of wood, and not two pieces joined together.

Only a passing notice need be given to the
fact that in some of the Epistles of the New
Testament, which seem to have been written
before the Gospels, though, like the other
Epistles, misleadingly placed after the Gospels,
Jesus is said to have been *hanged* upon a *tree.*[1]
For in the first place the Greek word translated
"hanged" did not necessarily refer to hanging
by the neck, and simply meant suspended in
some way or other.   And in the second place
the word translated "tree," though that always
used in referring to what is translated as the
"*Tree* of Life," signified not only "tree" but
also "wood."

It should be noted, however, that these five
references of the Bible to the execution of Jesus
as having been carried out by his suspension
upon either a tree or a piece of timber set in
the ground, in no wise convey the impression
that two pieces of wood nailed together in the
form of a cross is what is referred to.

Moreover, there is not, even in the Greek
text of the Gospels, a single intimation in
the Bible to the effect that the instrument

---

[1] *Gal.* iii. 13 ; 1 *Pet.* ii. 24 ; *Acts* v. 30 ; *Acts* x. 39 ; *Acts* xiii. 29.

actually used in the case of Jesus was cross-shaped.

Had there been any such intimation in the twenty-seven Greek works referring to Jesus, which our Church selected out of a very large number and called the "New Testament," the Greek letter *chi*, which was cross-shaped, would in the ordinary course have been referred to; and some such term as *Katà chiasmon*, "like a chi," made use of.

It should also be borne in mind that though the Christians of the first three centuries certainly made use of a transient sign of the cross in the non-Mosaic initiatory rite of baptism and at other times, it is, as will be shown in the next two chapters, admitted that they did not use or venerate it as a representation of the instrument of execution upon which Jesus died.

Moreover, if in reply to the foregoing it should be argued that as it is well known that cross-shaped figures of wood, and other lasting representations of the sign or figure of the cross, were not venerated by Christians until after the fateful day when Constantine set out at the head of the soldiers of Gaul in his famous march against Rome; and that the Christian crosses

of the remainder of the fourth century were
representations of the instrument of execution
upon which Jesus died ; a dozen other objec-
tions present themselves if we are honest enough
to face the fact that we have to show that they
were so from the first.   For the Gauls, and
therefore the soldiers of Gaul, venerated as
symbols of the Sun-God and Giver of Life and
Victory the cross of four equal arms, ✛ , or
✕ , and the solar wheel, ⊕ or ⊕; while
the so-called cross which Constantine and his
troops are said to have seen above the midday
sun was admittedly the monogram of Christ,
⊕ or ⊕, which was admittedly an adaptation of the solar wheel, as will be shown
further on ; and it was as tokens of the conquest
of Rome by his Gaulish troops, that Constantine, as their leader, erected one of these symbols in the centre of the Eternal City, and
afterwards placed upon his coins the crosses
⊕,   ⊕,   ⊕,   ⊕,   ✳,   ✳,   ✚,
the cross of four equal arms ✕ , and several
variations of that other cross of four equal arms,
the right-angled ✛ .   And it was not till long
after these crosses were accepted as Christian,

and Constantine was dead and buried, that the cross with one of its arms longer than the other three (or two), which alone could be a representation of an instrument of execution, was made use of by Christians.

Another point to be remembered is that when Constantine, apparently conceiving ours, as the only non-national religion with ramifications throughout his world-wide dominions, to be the only one that could weld together the many nations which acknowledged his sway, established Christianity as the State Religion of the Roman Empire, the Church to which we belong would naturally have had to accept as its own the symbols which Constantine had caused to be those of the State in question. And it should be added that the cross of later days with one of its arms longer than the others, if not also the assumption that the stauros to which Jesus was affixed had a cross-bar, may have been merely the outcome of a wish to associate with the story of Jesus these Gaulish symbols of victory which had become symbols of the Roman State, and therefore of its State Church.

Anyway, the first kind of cross venerated by

Christians was not a representation of an instrument of execution ; and the fact that we hold sacred many different kinds of crosses, although even if we could prove that the stauros to which Jesus was affixed had a cross-bar but one kind could be a representation of that instrument of execution, has to be accounted for.

Our only plausible explanation of the fact that we hold sacred almost any species of cross is that, as we do not know what kind of cross Jesus died upon, opinions have always differed as to which was the *real* cross.

This difference of opinion among Christians as to the shape of the instrument upon which Jesus was executed, has certainly existed for many centuries. But as an explanation of the many different kinds of crosses accepted by us as symbols of the Christ, it only lands us in a greater difficulty. For if we did not know what kind of cross Jesus died upon when we accepted the cross as our symbol, the chances obviously are that we accepted the cross as our symbol for some other reason than that we assert.

As a matter of fact our position regarding

the whole matter is illogical and unsatisfactory, and we ought to alter it by honestly facing the facts that we cannot satisfactorily prove that our symbol was adopted as a representation of the instrument of execution to which Jesus was affixed, and that we do not even know for certain that the instrument in question was cross-shaped.

It need only be added that there is not a single sentence in any of the numerous writings forming the New Testament, which, in the original Greek, bears even indirect evidence to the effect that the stauros used in the case of Jesus was other than an ordinary stauros; much less to the effect that it consisted, not of one piece of timber, but of two pieces nailed together in the form of a cross.

Taking the whole of the foregoing facts into consideration, it will be seen that it is not a little misleading upon the part of our teachers to translate the word stauros as "cross" when rendering the Greek documents of the Church into our native tongue, and to support that action by putting "cross" in our lexicons as the meaning of stauros without carefully explaining that that was at any rate not the

primary meaning of the word in the days of
the Apostles, did not become its primary signification till long afterwards, and became so
then, if at all, only because, despite the absence
of corroborative evidence, it was for some reason
or other assumed that the particular stauros
upon which Jesus was executed had that
particular shape.

But—the reader may object—how about the
Greek word which in our Bibles is translated
as " crucify " or " crucified ? " Does not that
mean " fix to a cross " or " fixed to a cross ? "
And what is this but the strongest possible
corroboration of our assertion as Christians
that Jesus was executed upon a cross-shaped
instrument ?

The answer is that no less than four different
Greek words are translated in our Bibles as
meaning " crucify " or " crucified," and that not
one of the four meant " crucify " or " crucified."

The four words in question are the words
prospēgnumi, anastauroo, sustauroō, and *stauroō.*

The word *prospēgnumi,* though translated in
our Bibles as " crucify " or " crucified," meant to
" fix " to or upon, and meant that only. It
had no special reference to the affixing of

condemned persons either to a stake, pale, or post, or to a tree, or to a cross; and had no more reference to a cross than the English word "fix" has.

The word *anastauroo* was never used by the old Greek writers as meaning other than to impale upon or with a single piece of timber.[1]

The word *sustauroō* does not occur in pre-Christian writings, and only five times in the Bible against the forty-four times of the word next to be dealt with. Being obviously derived in part from the word stauros, which primarily signified a stake or pale which was a single piece of wood and had no cross-bar, *sustauroō* evidently meant affixion to such a stake or pale. Anyhow there is nothing whatever either in the derivation of the word, or in the context in either of the five instances in which it occurs, to show that what is referred to is affixion to something that was cross-shaped.

The word *stauroō* occurs, as has been said, forty-four times; and of the four words in question by far the most frequently. The meaning of this word is therefore of special

---

[1] *e.g.,* Hdt. iii. 125.

importance. It is consequently most significant
to find, as we do upon due investigation, that
wherever it occurs in the pre-Christian classics
it is used as meaning to impalisade, or stake,
or affix to a pale or stake; and has reference, not to crosses, but to single pieces of
wood.[1]

It therefore seems tolerably clear (1) that
the sacred writings forming the New Testament,
to the statements of which—as translated for
us—we bow down in reverence, do not tell us
that Jesus was affixed to a cross-shaped instrument of execution; (2) that the balance of
evidence is against the truth of our statements
to the effect that the instrument in question was
cross-shaped, and our sacred symbol originally
a representation of the same; and (3) that we
Christians have in bygone days acted, and, alas!
still act, anything but ingenuously in regard to
the symbol of the cross.

This is not all, however. For if the unfortu
nate fact that we have in our zeal almost
manufactured evidence in favour of the theory
that *our* cross or crosses had its or their origin

---

[1] *e.g.*, Thuc. vii. 25.

in the shape of the instrument of execution to which Jesus was affixed proves anything at all, it proves the need for a work which, like the present one, sets in array the evidence available regarding both the pre-Christian cross and the adoption in later times of a similar symbol as that of the catholic faith.

Nor should it be forgotten that the triumph of Christianity was due to the fact that it *was* a " catholic " faith, and not, like the other faiths followed by the subjects of Rome, and like what Jesus seems to have intended the results of His mission to have been inasmuch as He solemnly declared that he was sent to the lost sheep of the House of Israel and to them alone, the monopoly of a single nation or race.

For if Paul, taking his and other visions of Jesus as the long-needed proofs of a future life, had not disregarded the very plain intimations of Jesus to the effect that His mission was to the descendants of Jacob or Israel, and to them alone; if Paul had not withstood Christ's representative, Peter, to the face, and, with unsurpassed zeal, carried out his grand project of proclaiming a non-national and universal religion founded upon appearances of the spirit-form of Jesus, what we call Christianity would not have come into existence.

The fact that but for Paul there would have been no catholic faith with followers in every land ruled by Constantine when sole emperor, for that astute monarch to establish as the State Religion of his loosely knit empire, because, on account of its catholicity, that best fitted to hold power as the official faith of a government with world-wide dominions, is worthy of a lasting place in our memory.

Nor is the noteworthy fact last mentioned unconnected with the symbol of the cross. For, as will be shown, it is clear that it was because Constantine caused the figure of the cross to become a recognized symbol of his catholic empire, that it became recognized as a symbol of the catholic faith.

Not till after Constantine and his Gaulish warriors planted what Eusebius the Bishop of Cæsarea and other Christians of the century in question describe as a cross, within the walls of the Eternal City as the symbol of their victory, did Christians ever set on high a cross-shaped trophy of any description.

Moreover, but for the fact that, as it happened,

the triumph of Constantine resulted in that of
the Christian Church, we should probably have
deemed the cross, if to our minds a representation of the instrument of execution to which
Jesus was affixed, as anything but the symbol
of Victory we now deem it.

This is evident from the fact that the so-called
cross of Jesus admittedly fulfilled the purpose
for which it was erected at the request of
those who sought the death of Jesus. And
even according to our Gospels the darkness of
defeat o'ershadowed the scene at Calvary.

To put the matter plainly, the victory of Jesus
was not a victory over the cross ; for He did not
come down from the cross. Nor was it a victory
over His enemies ; for what they sought was
to get rid of a man whom they deemed an agita-
tor, and their wish was gratified, inasmuch as,
thanks to the cross, He troubled them no more.

In other words the victory which we ascribe
to Jesus did not occur during the gloom which
hung like a pall over his native land at the
time of His execution, but upon the then
approaching Sun-day of the Vernal Equinox,
at the coming of the glory of the dawn.

For the victory in question, from whatever

point of view we may look at it, was not the avoidance of defeat, but its retrieval. And its story is an illustration of the old-world promise, hoary with antiquity and founded upon the coming, ushered in every year by the Pass-over or cross-over of the equator by the sun at the Vernal Equinox, of the bounteous harvests of summer after the dearth of devastating winter ; bidding us ever hope, not indeed for the avoidance of death and therefore of defeat, but for such victory as may happen to lay in survival or resurrection.

It is therefore clear that even if we *could* prove that the instrument of execution to which Jesus was affixed was cross-shaped, it would not necessarily follow that it was as the representation of the cause of His death which we now deem it, that the figure of the cross became our symbol of Life and Victory.

In any case honesty demands that we should no longer translate as " cross " a word which at the time our Gospels were written did not necessarily signify something cross-shaped. And it is equally incumbent upon us, from a moral point of view, that we should cease to render as " crucify " or " crucified " words which never bore any such meaning.

CHAPTER II.

THE Fathers who wrote in Latin, used word *crux* as a translation of the Greek word *stauros*. It is therefore noteworthy that even this Latin word "crux," from which we derive our words "cross" and "crucify," did not in ancient days necessarily mean something cross-shaped, and seems to have had quite another signification as its original meaning.

A reference, for instance, to the writings of Livy, will show that in his time the word crux, whatever else it may have meant, signified a single piece of wood or timber; he using it in that sense.[1]

This however is a curious rather than an important point, for even the assumption that the word *crux* always and invariably meant

---

[1] Livy, xxviii. 29.

mething cross-shaped, would not affect the demonstration already made that the word *stauros* did not.

As our Scriptures were written in Greek and were written in the first century A.C., the vital question is what the word stauros then meant, when used, as in the New Testament, without any qualifying expression or hint that other than an ordinary stauros was signified. What the Fathers chose to consider the meaning of that word to be, or [chose to give as its Latin translation, would, even if they had written the same century, in no wise affect that issue. And, as a matter of fact, even the earliest of the Fathers whose undisputed works have come down to us, did not write till the middle of the second century.

Granting, however, as all must, that most if not all of the earlier of the Fathers, and certainly all the later ones, rightly or wrongly interpreted the word stauros as meaning something cross-shaped, let us, remembering that this does not dispose of the question whether they rightly or wrongly so interpreted it, in this and the next two chapters pass in review the references to the cross made by the Fathers

who lived before Constantine's march upon
Rome at the head of his Gaulish army.

Commencing, on account of its importance,
with the evidence of Minucius Felix, we find
that this Father wrote

"We assuredly see the sign of a cross naturally, in
the ship when it is carried along with swelling sails,
when it glides forward with expanded oars ; and when
the military yoke is lifted up it is the sign of a cross ;
and when a man adores God with a pure mind, with
arms outstretched.   Thus the sign of the cross either
is sustained by a natural reason or your own religion
is formed with respect to it."[1]

Various other pronouncements to a similar
effect are to be found in the writings of other
Christian Fathers, and such passages are often
quoted as conclusive evidence of the Christian
origin of what is now our symbol.   In reality,
however, it is somewhat doubtful if we can
fairly claim them as such; for the question
arises whether, if the writers in their hearts
believed their cross to be a representation of the
instrument of execution to which Jesus was
affixed, they would have omitted, as they did
in every instance, to mention that as the right

---

[1] Minucius Felix, *Oct.* xxix.

and proper and all-sufficient reason for venerating the figure of the cross.

Moreover it is quite clear that while, as will be shown hereafter, the symbol of the cross had for ages been a Pagan symbol of Life, it can, as already stated, scarcely be said to have become a Christian *symbol* before the days of Constantine. No ross-shaped symbol of wood or of any other material had any part in the Christianity of the second and third centuries; and the only cross which had any part in the Christianity of those days was the immaterial one traced upon the forehead in the non-Mosaic and originally Pagan initiatory rite of Baptism, and at other times also according to some of the Fathers, apparently as a charm against the machinations of evil spirits.

This " sign " or " signal " rather than " symbol " of the cross, referred to as theirs by the Christian writers of the second and third centuries, is said to have had a place before our era in the rites of those who worshipped Mithras, if not also of those who worshipped certain other conceptions of the Sun-God ; and it should be noted that the Fathers insist upon it that a similar mark is what the prophet

Ezekiel referred to as that to be placed upon the foreheads of certain men as a sign of life and salvation; the original Hebrew reading "Set a *tau* upon the foreheads of the men" (*Ezek.* ix. 4), and the tau having been in the days of the prophet in question—as we know from relics of the past—the figure of a cross. Nor should it be forgotten that Tertullian admits that those admitted into the rites of the Sun-God Mithras were so marked, trying to explain this away by stating that this was done in imitation of the then despised Christians![1]

That it was this immaterial sign or signal, rather than any material symbol of the cross, which Minucius Felix considered Christian, is demonstrated by the fact that the passage already quoted is accompanied by the remark that

"Crosses, moreover, we Christians neither venerate nor wish for. You indeed who consecrate gods of wood venerate wooden crosses, perhaps as parts of your gods. For your very standards, as well as your banners, and flags of your camps, what are they but crosses gilded and adorned? Your victorious trophies not only imitate the appearance of a simple cross, but also that of a man affixed to it."[2]

---

[1] *De Praescrip.* xl. [2] *Oct.* xxix.

This remarkable denunciation of the Cross as a Pagan symbol by a Christian Father who lived as late as the third century after Christ, is worthy of special attention; and can scarcely be said to bear out the orthodox account of the origin of the cross as a Christian symbol. It is at any rate clear that the cross was not our recognised symbol at that date; and that it is more likely to have been gradually adopted by us from Sun-God worshippers, than by the worshippers of Mithras and other pre-Christian conceptions of the Sun-God from us.

As our era was six or seven centuries old before the crucifix was introduced, and the earliest pictorial representation of the execution of Jesus still existing or referred to in any work as having existed was of even later date, much stress has been laid by us upon what we allege to be a caricature of the crucifixion of Jesus and of much earlier date. The drawing in question was discovered in 1856 to be scrawled upon a wall of the Gelotian House under the Palatine at Rome; and as no Christian representations of the alleged execution upon a cross-shaped instrument of even a reasonably early date exist, it would of course be greatly to our

interest to be able to quote this alleged caricature, which is said to be as old as the third
and perhaps even as old as the second century,
as independent evidence of the truth of our
story.   But can we fairly do so ?

The drawing in question is a very roughly
executed representation of a figure with human
arms, legs, and feet ; but with an animal's head.
The arms are extended ; and two lines, which
are said to represent a cross but appear in
front of the figure instead of behind it, traverse
the arms and trunk.   In the foreground is a
man looking at this grotesque figure ; and an
accompanying inscription is to the effect that
" Alexamenos adores his God."

Tertullian relates that a certain Jew " carried
about in public a caricature of us with this
label, *An ass of a priest.*   This figure had an
ass's ears, and was dressed in a toga with a
book ; having a hoof on one of his feet." [1]

It is upon the strength of this passage and
the two lines traversing the figure, that we,
ignoring the fact that the figure is standing, claim
this much-quoted *graffito* as conclusive evidence

---

[1] *Ad Nationes,* xiv.

of the historical accuracy of our story.   But it may
be pointed out that even if this was a caricature
of the execution of Jesus made at the date
mentioned, a caricature, made certainly not less
than two hundred years after the event, is not
altogether trustworthy evidence as to the details.

And, was it a caricature of the execution of
Jesus?   It would appear not.

To commence with, the two lines or scratches
—for they are little more—which we call a
cross, need not necessarily have formed a part
of the original *graffito;* and, even if they did,
of themselves prove nothing.   There is no
reference to a cross in the inscription, nor is
there anything to show that an execution of
any kind is what is illustrated.   Moreover, the
hoof upon one foot, mentioned by Tertullian, is
not to be seen ; a remark which also applies to
the toga and the book he mentions.   And even
what Tertullian referred to was not a caricature
of the execution of Jesus.

It should also be noted that the head of the
figure in this famous graffito, is more like that
of a jackal than that of an ass ; and appears to
have been a representation of the Egyptian god
Anubis, who is so often to be seen upon relics

of the past as a figure with a jackal's head, with human arms extended, and with human legs and feet, as in this drawing.

Upon all points, therefore, our claim concerning the graffito is an ill-founded one ; and it cannot be considered evidence regarding either cross or crucifixion.

There thus being no opposing evidence of any weight, it is quite clear from the fact that as late as the third century after Christ we find a Christian Father who venerated the sign or figure of the cross denouncing it as a symbol, that no material representations of that sign or figure were recognised as Christian till an even later date. And such a conclusion is borne out by the striking fact that when Clement of Alexandria at the beginning of the third century made out a list of the symbols which Christians were permitted to use, he mentioned the Fish and the Dove but said nothing regarding the Cross. [1]

As to the sign or figure of the cross referred to by the Fathers of the second and third centuries, even so high an authority as the Dean of Canterbury admits, as we shall see in the next

---

[1] *Pæd.* iii. 11, 59.

chapter, that it was not "mainly" as reminding them of the death of Jesus that the Christians of the second and third centuries venerated it. If, therefore, not in the main, and, it would follow, not originally as a representation of the instrument of execution upon which Jesus died, what more likely than that the early Christians venerated the sign and figure of the cross as the age-old and widely accepted symbol of Life and of the Sun-God we know it to have been?

Anyway Minucius Felix may be said to stand alone in denouncing the symbol of the cross as non-Christian. And as even he expresses veneration for the figure of the cross, and must have approved of the sign of the cross in the initiatory rite of baptism, that denunciation evidently applied only to material representations of the cross.

Moreover the denunciation in question was clearly due to the fear that such objects might degenerate amongst Christians, as they afterwards did, into little better than idols. And if the sign or figure of the cross did not mainly remind the early Christians of the death of Jesus, it must have mainly reminded them of something else.

CHAPTER III.

THE EVIDENCE OF THE OTHER FATHERS.

THE works which have come down to us from the Fathers who lived before the days of Constantine make up over ten thousand pages of closely printed matter ; and the first point which strikes those who examine that mass of literature with a view to seeing what the Christians of the first three centuries thought and wrote concerning the execution of Jesus and the symbol of the cross, is that the execution of Jesus was hardly so much as mentioned by them, and no such thing as a representation of the instrument of execution once referred to.

Another fact worthy of special note is that, whether the Fathers wrote in Greek and used the word *stauros*, or wrote in Latin and translated that word as *crux*, they often seem to have had in their mind's eye a tree; a tree which moreover was closely connected in meaning with the forbidden tree of the Garden of Eden, an allegorical figure of undoubtedly phallic signification which had its counterpart in the Tree of the Hesperides, from which the Sun-God Hercules after killing the Serpent was fabled to have picked the Golden Apples of Love, one of which became the symbol of Venus, the Goddess of Love. Nor was this the only such counterpart, for almost every race seems in days of old to have had an allegorical Tree of Knowledge or Life whose fruit was Love; the ancients perceiving that it was love which produced life, and that but for the sexual passion and its indulgence mankind would cease to be.

Starting upon an examination of the early Christian writings in question, we read in the *Gospel of Nicodemus* that when the Chief Priests interviewed certain men whom Jesus had raised from the dead, those men made upon their faces "the sign of the stauros." [1] The sign of the cross is presumably meant; and

---

[1] *Nicodemus* i.

all that need be said is that if the men whom
Jesus raised from the dead were acquainted
with the sign of the cross, it would appear
that it must have been as a pre-Christian
sign.

Further on in the same Gospel, Satan is
represented as being told that " All that thou
hast gained through the Tree of Knowledge,
all hast thou lost through the Tree of the
Stauros." [1]

Elsewhere we read that " The King of Glory
stretched out his right hand, and took hold of
our forefather Adam, and raised him : then,
turning also to the rest, he said, Come with me
as many as have died through the Tree which
he touched, for behold I again raise you all up
through the Tree of the Stauros." [2]   Some see
in this peculiar pronouncement a reference to the
doctrine of re-incarnation.

In the *Acts and Martyrdom of the Holy
Apostle Andrew* we are told that those who
executed Andrew " lifted him up on the stauros,"
but " did not sever his joints, having received
this order from the pro-consul, for he wished him

---

[1] *Nicodemus* vii.   [2] *Nicodemus* viii.

to be in distress while hanging, and in the night-
time as he was suspended to be eaten by dogs."
There is nothing to show that the stauros used
was other than an ordinary stauros.

In the *Epistle of Barnabas* are various references to the stauros ; mixed up with various
passages from the Hebrew Scriptures, quoted—
without any justification—as referring to the
initiatory rite of baptism ; a rite, be it noted,
that was admittedly of Gentile rather than
Israelitish origin, and not unconnected with the
Sun-God worship of the Persians and other
Orientals of non-Hebrew race.

The references in question commence with the
enquiry, " Let us further ask whether the Lord
took any care to foreshadow the Water and the
Stauros ? "

Afterwards we have a quotation of *Psalm* i.
3-6—which likens the good man to a tree planted
by the side of a river and yielding his fruit in
due season—and the pronouncement, " Mark how
he has described at once both the Water and the
Stauros. For these words imply, Blessed are
they who, placing their trust in the Stauros, have
gone down into the Water."

This   further   reference   to   the   non-Mosaic

initiatory rite of baptism is followed by a
quotation of *Ezekiel* xlvii. 12, which speaks of
a river by whose side grow trees those who eat
the fruit of which grow for ever.

Further on is a declaration that when Moses
stretched out his hands (in a direction not speci-
fied) that victory might rest with the forces he
commanded, he stretched them out in the figure
of a stauros, as a prophecy that Jesus " would be
the author of life."

A reference is then made to the Brazen Serpent, and to the pole upon which it was placed ;
and it is stated that this lifeless imitation of a
serpent was a type of Jesus.

In the *Epistle of Ignatius to the Ephesians* we
read that the stauros of the Christ is indeed a
stumbling block to those who do not believe.

The evidence of Irenæus, as that of one who
was through his acquaintance with the aged Polycarp almost in touch as it were with the apostles,
will on account of his importance as a witness
be specially dealt with in the next chapter.

Justin Martyr, arguing that the figure of the
cross is impressed upon the whole of nature,
asks men to

" Consider all things in the world, whether without

this form they could be administered or have any certainty. For the sea is not traversed except that trophy
which is called a sail abide safe in the ship ; and the
earth is not ploughed without it : diggers and mechanics
do not their work except with tools which have this
shape. And the human form differs from that of the
irrational animals in nothing else than in its being erect
and having the hands extended and having on the face
extending from the forehead what is called the nose,
through which there is respiration for the living creature ;
and this shows no other form than that of the cross.
And so it was said by the prophet *The breath before our
face is the Lord Christ.* And the power of this form
is shown by your own symbols on what are called
standards and trophies ; with which all your proces-
sions are made, using these as insignia of your power
and government." [1]

Elsewhere Justin Martyr declares that the
Christ

"Was symbolised both by the Tree of Life which was
said to have been planted in Paradise, and by those
events which should happen to all the just. Moses was
sent with a *rod* to effect the redemption of the people ;
and with this in his hands at the head of the people he
divided the sea. By this he saw the water gushing out
of the rock ; and when he cast a *tree* into the waters of
Marah, which were bitter, he made them sweet. Jacob
by putting *rods* into the water troughs caused the sheep

---

[1] *Apol.* i. 55.

of his uncle to conceive . . . . Aaron's *rod* which blossomed declared him to be the High Priest. Isaiah prophesied that a *rod* would come forth from the root of Jesse, and this was the Christ." [1]

Further on in the same work, Justin Martyr, alluding to the statement in the Israelitish Law "Cursed is every one that hangeth on a tree," states that

"It was not without design that the prophet Moses when Hur and Aaron upheld his hands, remained in this form until evening. For indeed the Lord remained upon the tree almost until evening." [2]

Tertullian writes concerning the Christ "With the last enemy Death did he fight, and through the trophy of the cross he triumphed" [3]; and elsewhere tells us that "Cursed is every one who hangeth on a tree" was a prediction of his death. [4]

There is also in existence a long essay by Tertullian which starts by discussing the efficacy of "the sign" as an antidote. The sign of the cross as traced upon the forehead in the non-Mosaic initiatory rite of baptism seems

---

[1] *Dial. cum Trypho*, lxxxvi. [2] *Dial. cum Trypho*, xcvii.
[3] *Against Marcion*, iv. 20. [4] *Against Marcion*, iii. 18.

to be what is referred to ; and no representation of an instrument of execution, or cross-shaped symbol of wood or any material, is once mentioned. [1]

In another of Tertullian's works we come across the passage " In all the actions of daily life we trace upon the forehead the sign." [2]

His famous reference to the Sun-God Mithras reads as follows :—

" The devil in the mystic rites of his idols competes even with the essential portions of the sacraments of God. He, like God, baptizes some, that is, his own believing and faithful followers, and promises the putting away of sins by baptism ; and if I remember rightly Mithras there signs his soldiers upon their foreheads, celebrates the oblation of bread, introduces a representation of the resurrection, and places the crown beyond the sword." [3]

Elsewhere Tertullian writes :—

" If any of you think we render superstitious adoration to the cross, in that adoration he is sharer with us . .
You worship *victories*, for in your trophies the cross is the heart of the trophy. The camp religion of the Romans is all through a worship of the standards . . . I praise your zeal : you would not worship crosses unclothed and unadorned." [4]

---

[1] *Scorpiace*, i.   [2] *De Corona*, iii.
[3] *De Præscrip*, xl.   [4] *Apologeticus*, xvi.

In another of Tertullian's works we read :—

"As for him who affirms that we are the priesthood of a cross, we shall claim him as a co-religionist . . . Every piece of timber which is fixed in the ground in an erect position is part of a cross, and indeed the greater part of its mass. But an entire cross is attributed to us . . . . The truth however is that *your* religion is *all* cross . . . You are ashamed, I suppose, to worship unadorned and simple crosses." [1]

In the *Instructions of Commodianus* we read " The first law was in the tree, and so, too, was the second." [2]

Cyprian contends that " By the sign of the cross, also, Amalek was conquered by Moses." [3]

Elsewhere Cyprian tells us that " In this sign of the cross is salvation for all people who are marked on their foreheads "; quoting as proof of this, from the Apocalypse, " They had his name and the name of his Father written on their foreheads," and " Blessed are they that do his commandments that they may have power over the Tree of Life." [4]

Methodius tells us that " He overcame, as has

[1] *Ad Nationes*, xii.   [2] xxxvi.

[3] *Testimonies against the Jews*, ii. 21.

[4] *Testimonies against the Jews*, ii. 22.

been said, the powers that enslaved us by the figure of the cross ; and shadowed forth man, who had been oppressed by corruption as by a tyrant power, to be free with unfettered hands. For the cross, if you wish to define it, is the confirmation of victory." [1]

Passing on to Origen, we find in one of his works the noteworthy passage :—

"It is possible to avoid it if we do what the Apostle saith ' Mortify your members which are upon earth,' and if we always carry about in our bodies the death of Christ. For it is certain that where the death of Christ is carried about, sin cannot reign. For the power of the *stauros* of Christ is so great that if it be set before a man's eyes and kept faithfully in his mind so that he look with steadfast eyes of the mind upon that same death of Christ, no concupiscence, no sensuality, no natural passion, and no envious desire, is able to overcome him." [2]

Whether however this reference to the "*stauros* of Christ" is or is not a reference to the figure of the cross, is doubtful.

Such is the evidence regarding the cross, whether considered as immaterial sign or material symbol, obtainable from the writings of the

---

[1] *Apud Gretserum*, ii.
[2] *Epist. ad Romanos*, Lib. vi.

Christians who lived between the days of the Apostles and those of Constantine; other of course than the *Octavius* of Minucius Felix, which was dealt with in the last chapter, and the writings of Irenæus, which will be dealt with in the next.

Among the noteworthy features of the evidence in question prominently stands out the smallness of its volume.

This is but a negative point, however; and what should be carefully borne in mind is that the evidence as a whole leads to the conclusion that the Christians of the second and third centuries made use of the sign and venerated the figure of the cross without, as Dean Farrar admits, it "only or even mainly," reminding them of the death of Jesus; and therefore otherwise than as a representation of the instrument of execution upon which Jesus died. [1]

---

[1] *Christ in Art*, p. 23.

CHAPTER IV

CURIOUS STATEMENTS OF IRENÆUS.

THE special importance of the evidence of Irenæus, is due to the fact that of all the Fathers whose undisputed works have come down to us he is the only one who can be considered to have been anything like in touch with the Apostles. As an acquaintance of the aged Polycarp, who is said to have been in his youth a pupil of the aged Evangelist and Apostle St. John and to have met yet other Apostles, Irenæus had opportunities for ascertaining facts concerning the life and death of Jesus which the other Fathers upon whose works we rely did not possess.

What, then, does this important witness have to say, which bears upon the points at issue? As a matter of fact, very little.

There are, however, two passages in the works of Irenæus which it would not be right to altogether ignore.

In the first of these passages Irenæus mentions that some Christians believed that Simon of Cyrene was executed instead of Jesus, owing to the power of Jesus to metamorphose himself and others having been exercised with that object in view. [1] This power is referred to more than once in our Gospels, for instance in the account of the so-called "Transfiguration" upon the Mount ; the Greek word rendered in our Bibles as "transfigured" being the word which in translations of the older Greek classics is rendered "metamorphosed."

Even if we pass by this belief of certain of the early Christians that Jesus was never executed, a question here arises which should at least be stated, and that is the question how, if Jesus was metamorphosed upon the Mount, as the Gospels tell us, he can be said to have died as a man at Calvary? For if upon the Mount of Transfiguration, or at any other time previous to the scene at Calvary, Jesus was

---

[1] *Against Heresies*, i. xxiv.

metamorphosed, the form which was the result of the process of re-metamorphosis necessary to make him recognisable again cannot be said to have been born of the Virgin Mary, and can have been human only in appearance.

The other passage in the writings of Irenæus which deserves our notice, is neither more nor less than an emphatic declaration, by Irenæus himself, that Jesus was not executed when a little over thirty years of age, but lived to be an old man. Explain it away how we will, the fact remains; and it certainly ought not to be ignored.

At first sight this statement of Irenæus would decidedly seem to support the theory advanced by some, that, as the Roman Procurator Pontius Pilate admittedly did not want to carry out the extreme penalty in the case of Jesus, though he reluctantly consented to do so in order to pacify the Jews and allowed Jesus to be fixed to a stauros and suspended in public view, he took care to manage things so that Jesus should only appear to die. The idea of course is that if Pilate wished to preserve the life of Jesus he could easily have had him taken down while in a drugged condition, have had the farce of burial carried out at the earliest possible moment, and then have had him resuscitated and removed to some region where he could dwell in safety.

What Irenæus says concerning Jesus is that

"He passed through every age, becoming an infant for infants. . . . So likewise he was an old man for old men, that he might be a perfect Master for all, not merely as regards the setting forth of the truth but also as regards age, sanctifying at the same time the aged also and becoming an example to them likewise. Then, at last, he came on to death itself.   From the fortieth and fiftieth year a man begins to decline towards old age, which our Lord possessed while he still fulfilled the office of a Teacher; even as the Gospel and all the elders testify, those who were conversant in Asia with John the disciple of the Lord affirming that John conveyed to them that information. And he remained among them up to the times of Trajan. Some of them moreover saw not only John but the other apostles also, and heard the very same account from them, and bear testimony as to the statement. Whom, then, should we rather believe? Whether such men as these, or Ptolemæus, who never saw the apostles and who never even in his dreams attained to the slightest trace of an apostle?" [1]

The reader must decide for himself or herself whether Irenæus believed that Jesus was never executed; or that he was executed but

---

[1] *Against Heresies*, II., xxii. 4-5.

survived ; or that he was born when we suppose, but executed thirty years or so later than we suppose ; or that, though executed when we suppose, he was then an old man, and was born, not at the commencement or middle or end of the year A.C. I, or B.C. 4, or whenever the orthodox date is, but thirty years or more before what we call our era began. Anyhow he mentions neither cross nor execution, and here seems to assume that Jesus died a natural death. And in any case the fact remains that, however mistaken he may have been, Irenæus stated that Jesus lived to be an old man ; and stated so emphatically.

Even granting that Irenæus must have been mistaken, his evidence none the less affects one of the most important points debated in this work. For it is clear that if even he knew so little about the execution of Jesus, the details of that execution cannot have been particularly well known ; and the affirmation that the stauros to which Jesus was affixed had a transverse bar attached may have had no foundation in fact, and may have arisen from a wish to connect Jesus with that well-known and widely-venerated Symbol of Life, the pre-Christian cross.

CHAPTER V.

ORIGIN OF THE PRE-CHRISTIAN CROSS.

HAVING in the foregoing chapters demonstrated that it is possible, if not indeed probable, that the instrument of execution to which Jesus was affixed was otherwise than cross-shaped ; and having also shown that it was not mainly, if indeed even partially, that the early Christians signified that instrument by the sign of the cross ; it is now desirable that, as a preliminary to an enquiry into the circumstances under which the cross became the symbol of Christianity, we should enquire into the origin of the *pre*-Christian cross.

That there was a pre-Christian cross, and that it was, like ours, a Symbol of Life, is generally admitted.

The authorities upon such subjects, however, unfortunately differ as to the reason why the

Cross came to be selected by the ancients as the Symbol of Life. And not one of their suggestions seems to go to the root of the matter.

Let us therefore in thought go back tens of thousands of years, and conceive the genus Homo as a race gradually awakening to reason but as yet unfettered by inherited traditions and creeds. Let us imagine Man ere he began to make gods in his own image. Let us remember that what would strike him as the greatest of all marvels would of necessity be Life itself, and that far and away the next greatest marvel must have been the glorious Sun; the obvious source of earth life, and Lord of the Hosts of Heaven.

Let us bear in mind, too, that though the Nature Worship of our remote ancestors had other striking features, the facts mentioned would lead to the predominance of the phallic idea, and to its association with Sun-God worship. And as Life, the greatest marvel of all, must have had a symbol allotted to it at a very early date, let us ask ourselves what the untutored mind of Man would be most likely to select as its symbol.

To this question there is, so far as the author can see, but one reasonable answer :—the figure of the cross.

And the author conceives this to be the real solution of the difficulty for this reason :—because the figure of the cross is the simplest possible representation of that union of two bodies or two sexes or two powers or two principles, which alone produces life.

For the ancients cannot fail to have perceived that all life more immediately proceeds from the *union* of *two* principles ; and the first, readiest, simplest, and most natural symbol of Life, was consequently one straight line superimposed upon another at such an angle that both could be seen ; in other words, a cross of some description or other.

It is evidently probable that this was the real reason why the figure of the cross originally came to be adopted as the Symbol of Life. But, of course, whatever the original reason, as time rolled on other reasons for the veneration of the cross were pointed out ; nothing being more natural than that primitive Man should, or more certain than that he did, find pleasure in connecting with other objects of his regard than

Life itself, that which as the Symbol of Life was pre-eminently a symbol of good omen.

The most notable instance of this is the way in which, or rather the different ways in which, the figure of the cross was connected with the Sun-God.

A good example of the last named fact, is the declaration of the philosophers of ancient Greece that the figure of the cross was the figure of the "Second God" or "Universal Soul," the *Ratio* as well as the *Oratio* of the All-Father, which they called the *Logos* of God; a term badly translated in our versions of the Gospel of St. John as the *Word* of God, as if it signified the *Oratio* only.

It was this Logos or "Second God" whom Philo, who was born before the commencement of our era, described as the "Intellectual Sun," and even as God's "First Begotten" and "Beloved" offspring, and the "Light of the World"; terms afterwards made use of by the writers of our Gospels in describing the Christ. And, as will be shown in a chapter upon the subject, the reason the philosophers, among whom was Plato, gave for declaring the cross to be the figure of the Logos, was that the Sun creates this figure by crossing the Equator.

An even better illustration can be seen in the fact that in days of old almost every civilised race held feasts at the time of the Vernal Equinox, in honour of the Passover or *Cross-over* of the Sun.

The fact that the ancients were thus at special pains to connect the symbol of Life with the Sun-God, and also, as we know, spoke of him as the "Giver of Life" and the only "Saviour," was doubtless due to their perceiving, not only that life is the result of the union of the two principles distinguished by the titles male and female, but also that the salvation of life is due to the action of the sun in preserving the body from cold and in producing and ripening for its use the fruits of the earth.

As the Giver of Life, the Sun-God was of course considered to be bi-sexual. But when the two great lights of heaven, the Sun and the Moon, were associated with each other, as was often and naturally the case, the Sun was considered to be more especially a personifica-tion of the Male Principle, and the waxing and waning moon, as represented by the Crescent, a personification of the Female Principle. Hence the worship of the God associated with the radiate sun, as of that of the Goddess associated with the crescent moon and called the Sun-God's mother or bride, was phallic in character; and their connection is repeatedly symbolised upon the relics which have come down to us from antiquity by the sign of the crescent containing within its horns either a disc or what we should consider a star-like object, which latter was almost as favourite a mode with the ancients of representing the sun as it is with us of representing a star or planet, as will be shown further on.

Returning, however, to the symbol of the cross, as the first and simplest representation of that union of the Male and Female Principles which alone produces what we mortals call life, it is extremely curious that the selection of the figure of the cross in comparatively modern times as the simplest and most natural symbol both of addition and of multiplication, should have led no one to perceive that, being for these very reasons also the simplest and most natural symbol of Life, a probable solution of the mystery surrounding the origin of the pre-Christian cross as a symbol of Life, as it were stared them in the face.

As to the contention of not a few authorities, apparently founded upon the mistaken assumption that the *Svastika* was the earliest form of cross to acquire importance as a symbol, that the pre-Christian cross was originally a representation of the wheel-like motion of the sun or a reference to the wheel of the Sun-God's chariot; it need only be remarked that evidence exists to show that the cross was a symbol of Life from a period so early, that it is doubtful if the Sun-God had then been likened to a charioteer, and not certain that either chariots or wheels had been invented. It is true that the Solar Wheel became a recognized symbol of the Sun-God, and that additional veneration was paid to it because the figure of the symbol of Life was more or less discoverable in the spokes allotted to the Solar Wheel; but it is putting the cart before the horse to suppose that the cross became the symbol of Life because its form was so discoverable.

It only remains to be added that there undoubtedly was a connection, however slight, between the pre-Christian Cross as the Symbol of Life, the Solar Wheel as a symbol of the Sun-God, and the Cross as the symbol of the

Christ.   And whatever the date at which the cross was first adopted as a Christian symbol, or whatever the reason for that adoption, there is no doubt that, as will be shown further on, our religion was considerably influenced by the facts that the Gaulish soldiers whose victories enabled Constantine to become Sole Emperor venerated the Solar Wheel, ⊛ or ⊕, and that their leader, who was anxious to obtain the support of the Christians, allowed a loop to be added to the top of the vertical spoke so that the Christians might be able to interpret the victorious symbol as ⊛ or ⊕, ☆ or ⳨ ; *i.e.*, XP or XPI, the first two or three letters of the Greek word XPIΣTOΣ, *Christos*, Christ.

CHAPTER VI.

ORIGIN OF THE CHRISTIAN CROSS.

A S has already been to some extent pointed out, it is evident that our beloved Christen dom more or less owes its existence to the fact that Constantine the Great when only ruler of Gaul, himself a Sun-God worshipper at the head of an army of Sun-God worshippers, seeing how greatly the small but enthusiastic bodies of Christians everywhere to be met with could aid him in his designs upon the attainment of supreme power, bid for their support. For to this politic move, its success, and Constantine's perception that only a non-national religion whose followers sought to convert the whole world and make their faith a catholic one, could really weld together different races of men, we owe the fact that when he became Sole Emperor he made Christianity the State Religion of the world-wide Roman Empire.

This act and its far-reaching effects, are not all we owe to Constantine, however. It should be remembered that even our creed was to some extent decided by him. For it was this Sun God worshipper—who, though he advised others to enter what he wished should become a catholic and all-embracing religion, refused to do so himself till he was dying—who called together our bishops, and, presiding over them in council at Nicæa, demanded that they should determine the controversy in the ranks of the Christians as to whether the Christ was or was not God, by subscribing to a declaration of his Deity. It is even recorded that he forced the unwilling ones to sign under penalty of deprivation and banishment.

From these and other incidents in his career it would appear that, either from policy or conviction, Constantine acted as if he thought the Sun-God and the Christ were one and the same deity.

The probability of this is more or less apparent from what we are told concerning the part he played in connection with what, thanks, as we are about to see, to him, became our recognised symbol.

Our knowledge of the part played by Constantine in connection with the symbol of the cross, except so far as we can gather it from a study of ancient coins and other relics, unfortunately comes to us solely through Christian sources. And the first that famous bishop and ecclesiastical historian Eusebius of Cæsarea, to whom we owe so large a proportion of our real or supposed knowledge of the early days of Christianity, tells us about Constantine and the cross, is that in the year A.C. 312—a quarter of a century before his admission into the Christian Church—Constantine and the Gaulish soldiers he was leading saw at noon *over the Sun* a cross of Light in the heavens, bearing upon it or having attached to it the inscription EN ΤΟΥΤΩ ΝΙΚΑ, *By this conquer.*

The words of the Bishop, who is reporting what he states the Emperor in question to have told him personally, are :—

"He said that at mid-day when the sun was beginning to decline he saw with his own eyes the trophy of a cross of light in the heavens, above the Sun, bearing the inscription EN ΤΟΥΤΩ ΝΙΚΑ ; he himself, and his whole army also, being struck with amazement at this sight " [1]

Though this marvellous cross, declared by Christian writers of that century to have been the so-called Monogram of Christ ⊕ or ⚹ or ⊕ or ⚼, appeared to an army of Sun-God worshippers, Constantine himself—as can be seen from his coins—remaining one for many years afterwards if not till his death, it is put before us as a Christian cross.

It is also noteworthy that no material representation of a cross of any description was ever held aloft by adherents of the Christian Church, until after Constantine is said to have had this more or less solar cross so represented as the standard of his Gaulish army.

Mention should therefore be made of the fact that, upon the coins he struck, the symbol ⊕ is perhaps the one which occurs the most frequently upon representations of the famous *Labarum* or Military Standard of Constantine; but that the symbol ⊕, the ⚹ and ⚼ without the circle, and the ⊗ and ✳, are also to be seen.

---

[1] *Vit. Const. I.*

Now the Gauls led by Constantine specially venerated the Solar Wheel. This had sometimes six and sometimes four spokes, ⊗ or ⊕, and the warriors of their native land had long been in the habit of wearing a representation of the same upon their helmets. It is therefore not improbable that even before the date of the alleged vision when marching upon Rome, some such symbol formed the standard of Constantine's army.

Anyhow, that the worthy Bishop Eusebius was, like other enthusiasts, liable to be at times carried by his enthusiasm beyond the limits of veracity, or else was the victim of imperial mendacity, is evident. For Eusebius tells us in the *Life of Constantine* he wrote after the death of his patron, that the night after this miraculous "cross" and motto were seen in the sky above the Sun, the Christ appeared to Constantine, and, showing the Gaulish general the same sign that had been seen in the sky, directed him to have a similar symbol made, under which his army—an army, be it remembered, of Sun-God worshippers—should march conquering and to conquer ! [1]

---

[1] *Vit. Const. I.,* 28, 29, 30.

All that is really likely to have happened is that Constantine, wishing to encourage his troops, bade them rally round a standard on which was represented the sacred Solar Wheel venerated by the Gauls; and that as with this as a rallying point Constantine and his Gauls became masters of Rome, the symbol we are discussing became a Roman—and therefore, later on, upon the establishment of our faith as the State Religion of the Roman Empire, also a *Christian*—symbol. And a loop seems to have been sooner or later added to the top of the vertical spoke of the Gaulish symbol, so that Christians could accept it as a Monogram of Christ; as has already been hinted, and as will be demonstrated further on.

A noteworthy point is that we have two accounts of Constantine's alleged vision of the Christ, and that they do not quite agree.

The Bishop of Cæsarea's account is, that the night after the Emperor—then only ruler of Gaul—and all his soldiers saw the " cross " and motto above the meridian sun, the Christ appeared to Constantine

" With the same sign which he had seen in the

heavens, and commanded him to make a likeness of that sign which he had seen in the heavens, and to use it as a safeguard in all engagements with his enemies." [1]

But the author of *De Mortibus Persecutorem,* a work said to have been written during the reign of Constantine, and attributed to Lactantius, refers to the alleged vision as follows :—

" Constantine was admonished in his sleep to mark the celestial sign of God on the shields, and thus engage in battle. He did as he was commanded, and marked the name of the Christ on the shields by the letter X drawn across them with the top circumflexed. Armed with this sign his troops—" [2]

and the differences between these two accounts are greater than would at first sight appear.

Let us however return to the story of the Bishop of Cæsarea, who tells us that the morning after the Christ appeared to Constantine, the Emperor told this second marvel to his friends, and, sending for the workers in gold and precious stones who are assumed to have accompanied the Gaulish army, directed them to overlay with gold a long spear

---

[1] *Vit. Const. I.,* 29.   [2] *De Mort. Pers.,* c. 44.

"On the top of the whole of which was fixed a wreath of gold and precious stones, and within this the symbol of the Saviour's name, two letters indicating the name of the Christ by means of its initial characters, the letter P being intersected with the letter X in its centre." [1]

Several questions naturally arise at this point of our enquiry, and it is not easy—nay, it is impossible—for us Christians to honestly dispose of all of them and yet retain our cherished opinions upon this matter. Only one such question need be stated, and it is this : Is it likely that the Infinite Ruler of the universe, either at mid-day or at mid-night, went out of his way to induce a Sun-God worshipper who would not enter the Christian Church till a quarter of a century later and ere then was to become a murderer of innocent persons like the boy-Cæsar Licinius, to adopt a symbol which he warranted would enable Constantine to lead on the Gauls to victory ?

Pursuing the narrative of Eusebius we find that he, alluding to the symbol which he describes as a monogram but calls a cross, states that, setting this "victorious trophy and salutary symbol" in front of his soldiers, Constantine

---

[1] *Vit. Const. I.*, 31.

continued his march against Maxentius ; and, with his forces thus " divinely aided," overthrew the Emperor just outside the Imperial City, entered Rome in triumph, and thanked God that He had enabled him to defeat and slay its ruler and assume the purple in that ruler's stead. [1]

Eusebius then tells us that Constantine, who did not dispose of all his rivals and become sole emperor till some twelve years later, as victor in the fight with Maxentius and master of Rome though not as yet of the whole empire, at once

" By loud proclamation and monumental inscriptions made known to all men the salutary symbol, setting up this great trophy of victory over his enemies, and expressly causing it to be engraven in indelible charac- ters that the salutary symbol was the safeguard of the Roman Government and entire people. Accordingly he immediately ordered a lofty spear in the figure of a cross to be placed beneath the hand of a statue representing himself in the most frequented part of Rome, and the following inscription engraven on it in the Latin tongue: ' By virtue of this salutary sign which is the true test of valour, I have preserved and liberated your city from the yoke of tyranny, and I have also set at liberty the Roman Senate and People, and have restored to them their ancient distinction and splendour.' " [2]

---

[1] *Vit. Const. I.,* 37.   [2] *Vit. Const. I.,* 40.

Now, as we have already seen, what Eusebius referred to as the "cross" observed above the mid-day sun (and accompanied by a miraculous inscription in, presumably, to agree with the monogram, the Greek language; which was, well, "Greek" to the Gaulish soldiers) was the so-called Monogram of Christ  or  or  or . That, too, was what Eusebius tells us the Christ afterwards told the Gaulish leader Constantine to model his military standard after. That, therefore, was the "salutary symbol" and "trophy of victory" referred to in the above passage from the same authority.

It is therefore clear that this "lofty spear in the figure of a cross" which Eusebius tells us was placed under the hand of the statue of Constantine in the central place of honour in Rome, was referred to by Eusebius as a "cross" because it was shaped like or in some way connected with some form or other of the so-called Monogram of Christ. And such a conclusion is borne out by the fact that spears with cross-bars had been in use among both Gauls and Romans for centuries, whereas this one is referred to as something out of the common.

It should also be noted that it was as a

victorious military standard, and not as either a monogram of the Christ or a representation of the *stauros* upon which Jesus was executed, that Constantine caused this ⊗ or ✳, or ⊕ or ✳, or ⊕ or ⊥ (all which variations occur upon the coins of Constantine and his successors), to become a symbol of the Roman Empire.

Further on in his history of the Emperor, Eusebius tells us that whenever Constantine saw his troops hard pressed, he gave orders that the "salutary trophy" should be moved in that direction, and that victory always resulted.

The Bishop of Cæsarea then goes on to relate that Constantine selected fifty men of his body-guard, the most distinguished for piety, valour, and strength, whose sole duty it was to defend this famous standard ; and that, of the elect fifty, those who fled were always slain, and those who stood their ground were always miraculously preserved. [1]

One would imagine from all this that there was only one labarum. Many different kinds are, however, represented upon the coins of

---

[1] *Vit. Const. II.* 7—9.

Constantine ; as also almost every variety of ordinary cross, except, perhaps, such as might conceivably have been a representation of an instrument of execution, like that which has since come into vogue among us.

Eusebius also tells us that Constantine caused to be erected in front of his palace a lofty tablet, on which was painted a representation of himself with the " salutary sign " over his head and a dragon or serpent under his feet. [1]

He also informs us that inside the palace and in the principal apartment, on a vast tablet in the ceiling, Constantine caused " the symbol of our Saviour's passion to be fixed, composed of a variety of precious stones inwrought with gold." [2]

Which of all the " salutary " signs that appear upon the coins of Constantine these particular crosses were, we do not know ; but it is, at any rate, obviously unlikely that a worshipper of Apollo who refused to enter the Christian Church till he was dying, and on his coins always attributed his victories to the Sun-God, elevated either as a representation of an instrument of execution.

---

[1] *Vit. Const. III.* 3.   [2] *Vit. Const. III.* 49.

As to the alleged finding at Jerusalem, by Helena the mother of Constantine, of three stakes with transverse bars attached, all of which were ancient instruments of execution and one of which was shown by the occurrence of a miracle to have been a cross to which Jesus was affixed three centuries before, it is clear that this is a fairy tale. The story cannot be traced further back than to St. Cyril of Jerusalem about A.C. 350; and Eusebius, who gives an account of Helena's visit to Jerusalem, does not mention any such occurrence as that in question; a sure sign that it was an invention of later date.

The Christian Church, however, in a weak moment vouched for the truth of this ridiculous story; and while what was suffered to remain in Jerusalem of the true cross became the treasure of that city and a trophy captured by its foes but afterwards secured from them and once more placed in its holiest shrine, what was broken up into relics for the faithful through-out Christendom multiplied into a thousand fragments; one of which forms the centre of the Vatican Cross, and such few others of which as survive would not if examined, 'tis said, even

6

prove to be all of the same kind of wood, or even limited to the two kinds for the presence of which a supposed cross-bar of another kind of timber might be held accountable.

The same Christian Bishop to whom this fairy tale can be traced, in a letter to one of the Emperors that succeeded Constantine declared that on the seventh of May A.C. 351 he and all the inhabitants of Jerusalem saw a brilliant cross in the heavens, stretching from Mount Golgotha to the Mount of Olives, and *shining like the Sun for several hours.* [1] And this marvellous vision is vouched for by St. Jerome, Socrates, Idatius, and the Alexandrine Chronicle, as well as by St. Cyril; and is still kept in memory by the Greek Church, a solemn festival being held upon anniversaries of the day in question. But which particular " salutary sign " thus shone in the sky like the Sun for hours, is uncertain.

These painfully obvious inventions cannot but incline broad-minded Christians to the belief that our Church went to great lengths in order to induce people to believe that the cross was

---

[1] *Opera S. Cyrilli* curâ Ant. Touttée 351 Menaeum Graecum ad diem 7 Maii.

essentially a *Christian* symbol; which tends to show that there was a danger of their thinking otherwise.

It is also clear from the evidence already quoted concerning the adoption by Christians in the fourth century of a symbol they denounced in the third, that whether Jesus was executed upon a cross-shaped instrument or not, that was not the chief reason why the phallic symbol of Life became recognised as the symbol of the Christ.

The striking fact that though, as will be shown, the cross of four equal arms (a cross which, as we have seen, preceded the Latin cross as a Christian symbol, and one form of which is still the favourite symbol of the Greek Church; while even in the other two great divisions of Christendom its numerous variations, wheel-like and otherwise, as a whole dispute the supremacy with the Latin cross) occurs many times upon the coins of Constantine, yet it was the so-called Monogram of Christ or adapted solar wheel of the Gauls which the Christians of the fourth century were most careful to claim as a Christian symbol, should also be noted. For though the cross of four equal arms was also put by

Constantine upon his coins as a solar symbol, yet that, being then, as for ages previously, a symbol of the Sun-God of world-wide acceptation, and one which as we shall see had already appeared as such upon Roman coins, it was not so much a Gaulish symbol as the other; and it was evidently because that other was the symbol followed by the triumphant leader of the Gauls and his victorious army, that the Christians wished to specially identify it with the Christ.

In any case, whether the so-called Monogram of Christ was more or less forced upon Christianity when Constantine made our faith the State Religion of his empire, or whether it was adopted by Christians of their own volition, it was a politic move (than which few possible moves could have done more to secure the triumph of our faith) to accept as the symbol of the Christian Church what was at one and the same time the symbol of Constantine, of the Roman State, and of the universally adored Sun-God.

That the more generally accepted symbol of the Sun-God, the cross of four equal arms, should in time supplant the more local one, was of course only to be expected; as was the adoption of a cross with one arm longer than the others, as being the only kind which could possibly be connected with the story of Jesus as the Christ incarnate.

As to the possible objection that what has been dealt with in this chapter has been rather the origin of the Christian custom of manufacturing and venerating material representations of the sign or figure of the cross than the origin of the Christian cross itself, the answer is obvious. And the answer is that the first cross which can *justly* be called "Christian," was the one which was the first to be considered, to use Dean Farrar's expressions, "mainly," if not "only," a representation of an instrument of execution · which cross was undoubtedly not a transient sign or gesture but a material representation of the cross with one arm longer than the others and was introduced after such representations of the cross of four equal arms and of the so-called Monogram of Christ had come into vogue among Christians as a consequence of the influence of Constantine.

CHAPTER VII.

THE ESTABLISHER OF THE CHURCH.

HAVING already shown not a little cause for believing that the adoption of the cross as our symbol is due to the fact that we Christians helped to secure the triumph of the ambitious ruler of the Gauls, and after receiving numberless smaller favours from Constantine during the years he was ruler of Rome but not as yet sole emperor eventually obtained from him the establishment of Christianity as the State Religion of the Roman Empire, adapting the victorious trophy of the Gauls and the various crosses venerated by them and other Sun-God worshippers to our faith as best we could, it is desirable that we should pause to trace the career of the man we hail as the first Christian Emperor.

To do this properly we must commence by referring to Constantine's father, Constantius Chlorus; and to the favour shown to Constantius Chlorus by his patron the Emperor Diocletian.

Finding the supreme rule of the almost world-wide Roman Empire too much for one man in ill-health to undertake successfully, Diocletian in the year A.C. 286 made Maximian co-emperor. And in A.C. 292 Diocletian followed this up by conferring the inferior position and title of Cæsar upon Galerius and Constantius Chlorus.

In A.C. 305 Diocletian relinquished power altogether, forcing Maximian to abdicate with him ; Galerius and Constantius Chlorus thus obtaining the coveted title of Augustus, and sharing the supreme power.

Galerius now ranked first, however ; for it was to the ruler of Illyricum and not to that of Gaul that Diocletian gave the power of appointing Cæsars to govern Italy and the East.

Constantius Chlorus died in Britain A.C. 306, the year after Diocletian abdicated ; and Galerius, who had married a daughter of Diocletian, naturally thought that under the circumstances he ought to become sole emperor.

The legions of Gaul, however, proclaimed

the son of Constantius Chlorus as Augustus in his stead ; and as Constantine thus became ruler of Gaul and a power to be reckoned with, Galerius thought it best to give way so far as to grant Constantine the inferior title of Cæsar.

Soon afterwards Galerius conferred the title of Augustus upon Severus ; and a little while after that the Eternal City was lost to Galerius through the revolt of his son-in-law Maxentius, the son of Maximian.

The Senate of Rome then asked Maximian to re-assume the purple, and he and Maxentius shared the power between them, both taking the title of Augustus.

Upon this Severus at the request of Galerius marched upon Rome. He was, however, defeated and slain.

After being more or less expelled by his son Maxentius, Maximian in the year A.C. 308 marched to Gaul and married his daughter Fausta to Constantine ; at the same time conferring upon him the title of Augustus.

About this time Galerius made his friend Licinius an Augustus in the place of Severus · whereupon Maximin, the Governor of Syria and

Egypt, demanded and was granted that title also.

There were thus in the year A.C. 308 some half-a-dozen Roman Emperors instead of one · there being Constantine and Maximian in the west, Maxentius at Rome, and Galerius, Licinius, and Maximin elsewhere; not to mention Diocletian, who was content to remain in retirement.

This decided break-up of the Roman Empire was Constantine's opportunity; and he was favourably placed, for he had a warlike and faithful people under him.

Moreover by reversing so far as lay in his power as ruler of Gaul the traditional policy of Rome towards Christianity, and setting himself forward as a champion of a non-national religion which had been persecuted because it was non-national, Constantine was secure of the enthusiastic backing of all the Christians to be found in the dominions of his various rivals.

In A.C. 310 Constantine either executed his father-in-law the Emperor Maximian, or caused him to commit suicide; and the first of his five rivals was disposed of.

In A.C. 311 the Emperor Galerius died from

disease, and Constantine's most formidable competitor, and one who undoubtedly had a better claim than himself to the position of sole emperor, thus opportunely made way for the ruler of Gaul.

In A.C. 312 Constantine marched at the head of the Gauls against the Emperor Maxentius, defeated him near the Milvian Bridge outside Rome, and entered the Eternal City in triumph. Maxentius is said to have been drowned in the Tiber ; and the Senate decreed that Constantine should rank as the first of the three remaining Augusti.

In A.C. 313 the Emperor Maximin fought the Emperor Licinius ; but his forces were defeated, and he soon afterwards died.

Some ten years or so later Constantine went to war with his only remaining rival, Licinius, defeated him, and became sole emperor, A.C. 324.

That despite his great qualities as a ruler the character of Constantine was not perfect, can be easily seen from the fact that, not content with executing the Emperor Licinius after accepting his submission, he murdered the young Licinius ; a boy certainly not over twelve years of age, and according to some authorities

two or three years younger than that. He
also put his own son Crispus to death, and
other relations as well.

We are told that Constantine was so tortured
by the memory of these and other crimes that
he applied to the priests of the Gods of Rome
for absolution, but that they bravely said that
there was no absolution for such sins, whereupon
this worshipper of the Sun-God turned to his
friends the Christians and they gave him what
he desired.[1]

This statement seems somewhat improbable,
however, as one would imagine that the Pagan
priests, when called upon by one who was
Pontifex Maximus and therefore their spiritual
superior as well as the supreme emperor, would
not have scrupled to invent some purifying rite
—if they had none such—warranted to blot out
the stain of every crime and thoroughly appease
offended heaven.

However this may have been, these terrible
crimes of Constantine, all committed many years
after his alleged conversion to our faith, show
how badly advised we are to so needlessly go

---

[1] Zosimus ii.

out of our way to claim as a Christian one who refused to enter the Christian Church till he was dying and possibly no longer master of himself.

It is said that this refusal of his to be baptised till he was weak and dying and surrounded by Church officials who would perhaps have spread the report that he had been baptised even if they had not then at last been able to induce him to take the decisive step, was due, not to want of belief, but to excess of belief; Constantine's idea being that the longer he put off the rite in question, the more crimes would it wash out. Or, in other words, that delay would enable him to sin with impunity a little longer.

This may possibly have been the case, but it should at the same time be borne in mind that whether Constantine called him Apollo or Christ, it seems probable that it was the Sun-God to whom he referred. For everything tends to show that this astute emperor, who so naturally wished to establish and mould a religion which all his subjects of whatever race or nationality might be reasonably expected to become in time willing to accept, acted during his reign as supreme ruler of the Roman World, if not from first to last, as if the Christ were but another conception of the Sun-God he was brought up to worship as Apollo and all countries venerated under some name or other.

This point is not only demonstrated by the fact that upon his coins Constantine repeatedly declared that the Sun-God was his invincible guide and protector and the giver even of the victory foreshadowed by the alleged vision of the cross or Monogram of Christ above the meridian sun, but is also clearly shown by certain incidents connected with the founding towards the end of his life of the new metropolis which in less than a century equalled Rome in all save antiquity.

New Rome, or, as we now call it, Constantinople, the city of Constantine, was built on the site of, and often called by the name of, Byzantium.   It was not designed till A.C. 324, and was not dedicated till A.C. 330, or, as some think, an even later date: Constantine dying in the year A.C. 337.

We are told that Constantinople was dedicated to the Virgin Mother of God.[1]   This should remind us of the fact that long before our era,

---

[1] Both Zonaras and Cedrenus bear testimony to this effect.

and right down to the time when Constantine selected Byzantium as the site of a new capital, that place was considered dedicated to the Virgin Queen of Heaven.

Now in the central place of honour in his new metropolis, one would naturally expect Constantine to erect something or other to the honour of the God to whom he attributed his victories.

Whose, then, was the statue Constantine towards the end of his life, and about twenty years after his alleged conversion to our faith, erected in the centre of the Forum of New Rome?

It was a statue of the Sun-God Apollo; or, as some explain it, a statue of himself adorned with the attributes of the Sun-God.

In fact, taking the career of Constantine as a whole, there is nothing inconsistent with the supposition that he was a Christian only in so far as, out of policy or conviction, he acted as if he considered the Christ to be one of many conceptions of the Sun-God. For although, as has been mentioned and will be shown in a later chapter, Constantine, upon the many varieties of coins he issued, repeatedly acclaimed the

Sun-God as his companion and the author of his triumphs, he never once, except in so far as he may have considered the God we Christians worship to be the Sun-God, so attributed his victories to the Christ.

CHAPTER VIII.

CROSS AND CRESCENT.

BEFORE passing in review the evidence regarding the symbol of the cross derivable from Roman coins and other relics of antiquity, a few introductory remarks are necessary regarding the too often forgotten fact that the ancients naturally looked upon the Giver of Life as bi-sexual; no life being known to them which was not a result of the conjunction of the Male and Female Principles.

The necessarily bi-sexual character of the creator of both the Male and Female Principles, was, it should be remembered, borne in mind by the thinkers of old all the while they accommodatingly spoke of the Sun-God or Giver of Life as being a personification of the Male Principle and gave him a Bride or Virgin Mother to represent the Female Principle.

Moreover, just as the disc of the Sun, or the star-like form which the ancients often used to signify the radiate or impregnating Sun, naturally came to be recognised as the symbol of the Male Principle, so the Crescent, as signifying the increasing Moon and the lesser of the two great lights of heaven, in like manner came to be adopted as the natural symbol of the Female Principle.

In this connection it will not be amiss to draw attention to the symbol of the conquerors of the city founded by Constantine. For though misleadingly called " the Crescent," that symbol is, as the reader cannot very well fail to be aware, not a mere crescent ; but one which has within its horns what we consider to be a star-like form and therefore call a star. And though it is possible that it was not knowingly adopted as such by the Moslems, this dual symbol was a combination of the ancient symbols of the Male and Female Principles.

An erroneous account of the origin of this symbol as a Moslem symbol is given in all our works of reference which deal with the matter, as if their compilers copied one from another without troubling to consider the evidence for themselves.

The incorrect but widely accepted explanation in question, is to the effect that the so-called *star* and crescent had its origin as a Moslem symbol in the capture of Byzantium or Constantinople by the Turks in A.C. 1453; our works of reference stating that it was then adopted by Mahomet II., as the symbol of the famous city he had taken from the Christians.

But was the "star and crescent" the symbol of the City of Constantine? It would appear not.

Ancient Byzantium was, as stated in a previous chapter, considered, long before our era and right up to the days of Constantine, as dedicated to the Virgin Queen of Heaven; whose symbol was a crescent. And when Constantine rebuilt and renamed Byzantium, he dedicated New Rome—or, as we now call it, Constantinople—to the Virgin Mother of God and Queen of Heaven; whose symbol, as can be seen upon reference to both ancient and modern representations of the Virgin Mary, is also a crescent. It would therefore appear that the symbol of the city is more likely to have been a simple crescent than the so-called *star* and crescent.

Such a conclusion is entirely borne out by

the evidence. For though the so-called star and crescent can be seen upon three or four coins struck at Byzantium before such a place as New Rome was thought of, this proves little if anything ; inasmuch as the symbol in question was a very common one in days of old, and occurs frequently upon coins struck elsewhere.

Moreover the question is what the symbol of Constantinople was at the time it was captured by the Turks. And an inspection of the coins issued by the Christian rulers of that city during the thousand years and more it was in their hands, will reveal to the enquirer that though the crescent with a *cross* within its horns appears occasionally upon the coins of the Emperors of the East, and in one or two instances we see a cross of four equal arms with each extremity piercing a crescent, it is doubtful if a single example of the so-called " *star* and crescent " symbol can be found upon them.

We learn from other sources also that the symbol of the imperial Christian Metropolis captured by the Turks nearly five hundred years ago and ever since retained by them, was a simple crescent. And there is no doubt whatever that the dual symbol of the Moslems was adopted by them, not when they brought about the downfall of Constantinople as a Christian city, but centuries before, as a result of the conquest of Persia.

It was in the year A.C. 641 that the battle of Nehavend, ever after called by the Moslems the *Victory of Victories*, laid at the feet of the followers of the Prophet the kingdom of Iran or Persia, and brought to an end the Sassanian Monarchy.

Now the coins of the Sassanian kings then and for the previous two centuries bore upon them, with scarcely an exception, the so-called "*star* and crescent"; and it was as the symbol of this Zoroastrian dynasty and of the fair land of Iran, that the Moslems adopted it as their own.

What the star-like object (star-like, that is, in *our* opinion) represented upon the coins of Iran or Persia when placed within the horns of a crescent, was, of course, the Sun. The supposition of certain writers that the dual symbol represented the two crescent-presenting orbs, Venus and the Moon, is entirely mistaken.

For though the conjunction of the two crescent-shaped and feminine lights of heaven, was of old, like the combination of the symbol of the Sun—as representing the Male Principle—with that ever feminine symbol the Crescent, held to signify Increase and Life, we are dealing with what was admittedly a Mithraic symbol. And not only was the star-like object in question the symbol of the Sun-God Mithras, but it was, as any student of the coins of the Sassanian dynasty can see, substituted for the disc.

Upon the Sassanian coins the so-called star, in reality a representation neither of a star nor of a planet but of the radiate Sun, seems to have been first substituted for the round disc as a representation of the Sun, by Perozes, about A.C. 457; the disc in the horns of a crescent being the symbol on the coins of his father Isdigerd II. and other predecessors. But the dual symbol miscalled the " star and crescent " was one even then of great antiquity, as will be shown in a later chapter dealing with Phœnician relics discovered in Cyprus and elsewhere.

The primary signification of the dual symbol in question, often accompanied on the Sassanian coins by a prayer that the monarch might " increase," or flourish generally, was undoubtedly *Life*. And it is clear that the conjunction of

the Crescent as the symbol of the Female Principle of Life with the star-like figure which
represented the radiate, life-giving, or impregnating Sun, must have not only signified Life,
but also the necessarily bi-sexual Giver of Life.

We are thus brought to the conclusion that
the Cross and the so-called Crescent are more
or less allied in signification.

Nor is this noteworthy fact to be wondered
at. For only words and forms divide the faiths
of Mankind, and at heart the one object of our
desires is Life. Even those who piously lay
down their lives for others here, do so in the
hope of being rewarded with longer life and
more blissful life hereafter.

Another point which is too often overlooked,
is that if the followers of the so-called Crescent
have, as would appear to be the case, forgotten
the meaning of their symbol and the fact that
it alludes to the bi-sexual nature of the Creator,
we followers of the Cross may all unconsciously
be in a very similar position regarding our
symbol. And as the Cross as the recognised
symbol of the Christ is not of older date than
the conquest of Rome by the Gàuls, and more
or less resulted therefrom, it is clear that the

same remark applies if we consider the Moslems to have adopted their symbol as that of the land they conquered from the Sassanian kings, rather than as one with the primal and natural interpretation of which they were content.

Anyway the cross as well as the " star and crescent " is more or less a bi-sexual symbol, as will be clear to those who understand how the cross came to be recognised ages before our era as the natural symbol of Life. And a good illustration of the fact in question still exists in the Caroccio crucifix of Milan ; in which relic we see, under the usual inscription, an androgynous Christ upon a cross, with a man's head but half the body of female form, and with, instead of a cloth or fig-leaf, the phallic *crux ansata*, or Egyptian cross or symbol of Life, placed sideways, and as if the oval represented the female organ of reproduction, and the *tau* or incomplete cross that of the other sex.

Like the Red Cross of to-day, the Caroccio bi-sexual crucifix, once so common in Italy, was a symbol of Life and Salvation in two senses ; it not only being considered so in itself, but being also used on the battlefield as a rallying point for wounded soldiers, signalling to them that bandages, drugs, and surgical aid, could be obtained where it towered aloft.

These references to the fact that in days of old many very naturally came to the conclusion that the Creator and Giver of Life and only Saviour must be bi-sexual, should remind us Christians that our assertion that the Infinite Spirit is "Our Father" is not from all points of view an improvement upon the ideas of the ancients. For they also, and rightly, conceived what we wrongly ignore, *viz.*, that the Infinite Author of all existence must also be "Our Mother."

In this respect Protestants have if possible gone even further astray than members of the Greek and Roman Churches. For in the veneration paid by the latter to Mary of Nazareth as the Bride of God, the Mother of God, the Star of the Sea, and the Queen of Heaven, can be seen a survival, however toned down or distorted, of the old idea that the Deity must necessarily be of both sexes.

Even the plainly evident fact that, while in pre-Christian days the symbol of the cross represented the two sexual powers in conjunction, it has in Christian times come to be considered

the symbol of Life as being the symbol of the
SON of God, should, moreover, lead us to note
that our religion scarcely does justice to the part
played in the economy of Nature by the fair
sex. This is doubtless due to the fact that the
moulding of our creed and the interpretation of
things hard to be understood has for the most
part been in the hands of the sex which, as the
author belongs to it, may by way of contrast be
called unfair.

Wheat, for instance, can be more unfair than
the assumption that God, if incarnated as one of
the genus Homo, must have been born a male?
Yet that assumption is at the very basis of
modern Christianity.

Moreover, even granting that the Deity was
specially incarnated in Jesus the Nazarene and
therefore as a male, why should we, as if supposing that a passing form could stamp its sex
upon an Infinite Spirit, speak of " God the Son "
yet never of " God the Daughter ? "

The fact is that the natural disabilities and
disadvantages of the childbearing sex have from
the first resulted in the power of the male sex
to rule the roast, and one result of the predominance thus ensured to the male sex by the

laws of Nature has of course been a similar predominance for the opinion that the Creator is of the male sex.

Some enthusiastic champion of her sex, alluding to the fact that the opposing sex now has a monopoly of the priesthood, may even go so far as to ask with a special meaning, Has not Man from the beginning made God in his own image?

The male sex did not always have a monopoly of the priesthood, however; and in few if any instances did the priests of old go so far as to teach that the Creator, whom out of compliment to the Deity—or themselves—they naturally spoke of as belonging to the stronger sex, was a male and *only* a male. Nor did they even assume such a thing. Though the different gods and goddesses were spoken of as belonging to this or that sex, more than one were regarded as in reality androgynous; and the fact that the Creator and Giver of Life must of necessity be so was very generally recognised.

As a matter of fact it is by no means certain that the Creator is not represented as being androgynous even in our Bible. For in the account of the Creation which the Jews brought

with them from Babylon, the Creator is represented as saying " Let *us* make man in *our*
image"; and a race which like the Jews solemnly
declared that there was but one God, could only,
it would seem, have accepted such a declaration
as a divine revelation if they conceived the God
supposed to be speaking to be androgynous, and
addressing the other part of himself. This
would account for the emphasis laid upon the
statem.ent that man was created " male *and*
female," like, or in the image of, the Creator.

In any case it is clear that if God be not
female as well as male, Man was *not* created in
the likeness of God.

The theory of the ancients that Man himself
was created an androgynous being, capable, like
the Creator, of creating life in himself, but was
afterwards divided into halves, one of which is ever
seeking to find the other, need only be mentioned.

Suffice it to add that it can scarcely be said
to have been altogether progress in the right
direction, which has led us mortals to call the
Author of all Life " Our Father," to the utter
obscuration of the equally important fact that
the Deity in whom we live and move and have
our being must also be " Our Mother."

CHAPTER IX.

THE CORONATION ORB.

THE fact that though we Christians fail to do the matter justice, the ancients upon the contrary recognised that the Creator and the Giver of Life cannot be rightly spoken of as belonging to one sex and one alone, is not the only fact which those who examine relics of antiquity, such as the coins of the Roman Empire, with a view to ascertaining what evidence is derivable from them that bears upon the history of the symbol of the cross, should ever bear in mind. Another point to be kept in view is the evolution of the Christian symbol now known as the Coronation Orb.

This compound symbol, which plays so prominent a part in the regalia of a Christian Monarch, also crowns the topmost height of many a Christian Temple; including both St.

Peter's at Rome and St. Paul's at London. And it is noteworthy that it bears a certain resemblance to the representation of the Apex, once worn by the Salian priests and afterwards by the Pontifex Maximus and the Flamens generally, which appears upon ancient coins of the *Fabia* gens ; the office of *Flamen Quirinalis* having been hereditary in the Fabia family.

Upon other coins also, what is said to be meant for the pontifical apex occurs as a round ball surmounted by something very like a cross, in the hand of a female figure representing Rome ; exactly as the so-called Coronation Orb is to be seen upon coins of later date in the hand of this or that Christian Emperor.

The evidence as a whole, however, favours the supposition that the Coronation Orb, instead of having been derived from the Apex of the Pagan priests and thus signifying the claim to priest-hood or headship of the church so often made by monarchs, is a development of the round object, frequently unsurmounted by anything, so con-tinually to be met with upon ancient coins of Rome in the hand of this or that God, Goddess, or Ruler.

This being the case, it is a matter of very

considerable importance that we should be quite
sure what the round object in question used to
signify, and should base our assurance upon
the results of personal investigation rather than
upon the assumption that the popular explanation is necessarily the correct one.

Though the round object in question was, as
stated, in days of old often used as a symbol by
itself, it was sometimes, and, as time rolled on,
more and more frequently, surmounted by a
small female figure with wings; which figure
was a representation of Victory. This figure
was, after the establishment of Christianity as
the State Religion of the Roman Empire,
gradually, and only gradually, supplanted by
the figure of the cross.

Although several writers of note assume that
the initiative in this direction was taken by
Constantine himself, the first step seems to have
been taken upon the death of Constantine, when
a coin or medal was issued on which the
deceased monarch is called a God and is represented as holding a round object surmounted
by the so-called Monogram of Christ ; a symbol
continually referred to by Eusebius and other
writers of the fourth century as a cross.

Later on an instance occurs of the Monogram surmounting a round object held by a female figure representing Rome. This is upon a coin issued by Nepotianus, a nephew of Constantine.

Passing on to the reign of Valentinianus II., we find that that Emperor issued a coin upon which a round object surmounted by a cross is to be seen in the hand of Victory herself. This would appear to have been the first instance in which what we should call a cross, supplanted the representation of Victory as a small female figure with wings, as a symbol surmounting the round object which we are considering.

A similar coin was issued by Theodosius I., surnamed the Great; the last of the Emperors of Rome whose rule extended throughout the whole of the Roman world.

The instances named are, it will be understood, the exceptions to the general rule during a considerable period. And upon many of the coins of the Emperors mentioned, as well as upon those of the intervening Emperors, the round object held by those rulers is surmounted by either a Victory or a Phœnix; usually by the former, but in several instances by the latter.

The first ruler who caused *himself* to be

represented as holding a round object surmounted by an ordinary cross, was Theodosius II., Emperor of the East.

The fact that for a long time the Victory,
the Phœnix, and the Cross, were made use of
as symbols which might be substituted one for
another, is worthy of special note. For the facts
that the round object held by Theodosius II.
is as often surmounted by a Victory as by a
Cross, and that a Victory instead of a Cross
was often used by succeeding Christian Emperors, tend to show that the Victory, the
Phœnix, and the Cross were allied in signification, and equally connected with the round
object the nature and meaning of which we are
about to enquire into.

The reader may possibly object that no case
has been made out for such enquiry, inasmuch
as not only did the cross in course of time
entirely supplant the Victory, but the round
object from first to last, and whether unsur
mounted by anything or surmounted by a
Victory or a Phœnix or a Cross, signified the
world upon which we dwell, the round world,
and nothing but the world.

Such is, of course, the popular assumption ;

based upon what we are taught in school books
and in standard works of reference. But, as a
matter of fact, in many cases the round object
admittedly signified an apple ; the Golden Apple
of the Hesperides : a well known phallic symbol.
Whenever a round object unsurmounted by anything is to be seen in the hand of either the
Sun-God Hercules or Venus the Goddess of
Love, it admittedly may have been, for it
admittedly often was, a representation, not of
the world, but of the Golden Apple. And not
only does it so occur upon a very large number
of coins, but in some instances we see the
Victory surmounting it ; recalling to our minds
the fact that victory, as signifying the triumph
of Life over Death, had a phallic as well as a
martial meaning, and is achieved every time that
a man is born into the world as a result of the
tasting of the fruit of the Tree of Life or of
the knowledge of good and evil.

Moreover, though the fact is now for some
reason or other ignored, the so-called Coronation Orb of Christian Monarchs was itself
once known as the Golden Apple. It is so
referred to in important Latin documents of
the Middle Ages ; for instance in the famous

8

Bull of Charles IV. regarding the Imperial elections, wherein we read of the right of the Counts Palatine of the Rhine to carry the symbol in question at the coronation of their Emperor. And to this very day the so-called Coronation Orb is known throughout Germany and Austria as *Reichsapfel*, the Imperial Apple.

It is therefore by no means certain that the round portion of the Coronation Orb which thus caused the name of "the Golden Apple" to be given to this compound Christian symbol, is not, like the cross above it, to some extent a phallic symbol.

Every one should know the classic story of the Golden Apple; how the tree which bore the Golden Apples grew up in the Garden of the Hesperides in honour of the wedding of Hera, a goddess who more or less personified the female sex; how the Golden Apples are variously said to have been dedicated to the Sun (Helios), to the Sun-God (Dionysos), and to the Goddess of Love (Aphrodite); how the Sun-God Hercules as one of the twelve labours which represented the months, slew the Serpent which guarded the tree, and plucked the fruit; and how the Goddess Eris, who alone of all the deities was not invited to the nuptials of Peleus and Thetis, revenged herself by throwing arr.ong the guests a Golden Apple inscribed "To the fairest," and Paris awarded it to the Goddess of Love, Aphrodite or Venus.

The story of the Garden of the Hesperides is at heart one with that of the Garden of Eden; for it is obvious that the same phallic meaning underlies each, and that they are but different versions of the same allegory.

It may here be called to mind that it has this century been discovered from the cuneiform inscriptions of Western Asia, that Eden was the name given by Babylonians in days of old to the plain outside Babylon, whereupon, according to the legends of that city, the creation of living beings took place. Also that much evidence has accrued which, impartially weighed in the balance, leads clearly to the conclusion that the all-important commencement of Genesis, which forms as it were the very basis of both the Jewish and the Christian Scriptures, was borrowed by the Jews from Babylon. And that it was in reality a *Babylonian* tradition or series of traditions of far older date than any writing of purely Jewish origin, has not only been amply proved by recent discoveries, but might indeed have been guessed from its reference to the Tower of Babel or Babylon.

Nor is this all, for among the age-old relics discovered in Western Asia is a pictorial representation of the allegorical Temptation and Fall.

Upon this noteworthy piece of evidence the Tree of Knowledge or Life, with which the figure of the cross was identified by the early Christians; the Serpent, which in all countries and every age has been more or less identified with the sexual powers; the Man; the Woman · and the Apple; are all represented. And it is important to note that, according to the cuneiform inscription upon another time-worn relic in the British Museum, the Babylonians of old, at a time when the descendants of Jacob or Israel were without scriptures of their own, had a tradition to the effect that the fate of our first parents—who, thanks to a wicked Serpent of Darkness, tasted of the forbidden fruit which grew in the " Garden of the Gods "—was placed in the hands of " their Redeemer."

It should also be pointed out that this voice from the dim and distant past distinctly states that the Redeemer in question was—the Sun-God.

In ancient days the so-called forbidden fruit or apple seems to have borne somewhat the same symbolic meaning that the egg did. But while the apple not only represented Life, but also, and primarily, that union between two sexes or principles which produces life, the egg more or less lacked the latter meaning, and, on the other hand, signified Existence in a wider sense than the apple did.

The *Cosmos* itself was an egg according to the conceptions of many of the ancients; and few ideas were more widely spread, or can be traced further back, than the one that the whole visible creation emerged from the original Chaos or Darkness in the shape of an egg.

The egg also, and above all, signified the Sun-God, as the acknowledged Giver of Life and Saviour of Life. Hence the prominent part which it played in the various religious mysteries of the ancients, and also the fact that the Egyptians represented the Sun-God Ra as giving forth such utterances as "I am the Creative Soul of the celestial abyss. None sees my nest, and none can break my egg." The egg referred to, was of course the Sun itself.

Even our Christian custom of exchanging

eggs at Easter is more or less derived from
Sun-God worship, being a survival from customs
practised long before our era at that particular
period of the year, the time of the Vernal
Equinox or Pass-over of the Sun, when the
Orient Light crosses the Equator to rise once
more in the Northern Hemisphere.

Nor are these the only facts connecting the
egg with Sun-God worship, for the Sun-God
Apollo was of old represented as born from the
egg of Leda, and the Sun-God Osiris was also
said to have been born from an egg.

Moreover the Chinese believe that the first
man was born from an egg, the Orphic hymns
speak of the " First-Begotten One " as " egg-
born," and the Greeks fabled that their Sun-God
Dionysos sprang from the cosmic egg.

As to the origin of the Coronation Orb, it is
noteworthy that no finer or more natural symbol
of Power could have been fixed upon than a
representation of that ball of fire which was so
frequently spoken of in bygone ages as " the
Orb," and from which all earthly life and power
may be said to proceed.

However the available evidence certainly seems
to show that the round object we are considering

is more likely to have signified the cosmic egg than the solar orb.

In any case the object in question cannot be shown to have represented the world upon which we dwell and that alone ; and nothing is more likely than that so famous a symbol should, like the cross which now adorns it, have more or less signified Life.

It should also be pointed out that this symbol of Power may have signified, not so much that the Ruler who used it laid claim to world-wide dominion, as that he held in his hand power over the lives of others ; and, possibly, also that he claimed to be, as the vicegerent of the Sun-God and Giver of Life, the only legitimate Saviour of his country.

The facts that the symbol was used in days of old by others than the Emperors whose sway extended over the whole of the Roman Empire, and is nowadays considered the rightful symbol of every Christian Monarch however limited the area over which his power is felt, should also be borne in mind ; though not of much value as evidence, as even petty rulers have been known to boast that they held the world in their grasp.

It should however be remembered that though

the ancients, struck by the dome-like appearance
of the sky and the circular movements of the
constellations, conceived the cosmos or universe
to be spherical, and in some instances even
constructed celestial globes upon which to record
the movements of Sun, Moon, Planets, and Stars,
it is doubtful if a single one of them considered
the world upon which we dwell to be spherical.
Also, that many a Christian Monarch has used
the Coronation Orb as a symbol of power, and
yet believed the earth to be otherwise than a
globe in shape.

In this connection it should be pointed out
that the round object which the ancients represented Atlas as supporting upon his shoulders,
usually in the presence of Jupiter, was not as is
vulgarly supposed the earth, but the heavens ·
Hesiod telling us that Atlas bore heaven with
his head and hands, Ovid that upon Atlas rested
heaven and all the stars, and other writers of
bygone ages that Atlas was a king who first
taught men that heaven had the shape of a
globe.

It is of course possible that the ancients may
have conceived the earth to be otherwise than
spherical, and yet, because the horizon which

appears to limit its extent seems to be circular,
or for some other reason, have considered a
round object to be a representation of it.

Even where, however, the ball-like symbol we
are considering may have represented something
other than the Golden Apple, the probability is
that it seldom if ever represented the earth.

For as, though the ancients may have conceived and spoken of the world we live upon as
being " round " in the same sense as a circular
coin is round, they did not think of it as being a
globe, it is obvious that the ball-like symbol in
question is much less likely to have signified the
—in their belief—non-globular earth, than it is
to have been a representation of something
which they did consider to be globular.

Such is the nature of the evidence which tends
to show that we Christians may be mistaken in
supposing that our famous symbol the Coronation Orb represents the round world upon which
we dwell, surmounted by the instrument of
execution upon which Jesus died.

Although, however, most points have now
been touched upon, including the important fact
that the so-called Coronation Orb of Christian
Monarchs used to be called, even by Christians,

the Golden Apple, the idea that it may have been the *crux ansata*, or Egyptian symbol of Life (an upright oval, perhaps signifying the female principle, set upon the top of the *tau*, or T cross, and thus turning into a complete cross what is really an incomplete one, and may be supposed to have signified the male principle) *reversed* (*e.g.*, *Archæological Journal* xlii. 164), should at least be mentioned. It ought, however to be pointed out that the Orb is even more like the ancient symbol of the planet sacred to Venus, the Goddess of Love, reversed.

Even this point does not exhaust the subject in hand ; for the fact that in days of old we used to represent the Christ as the Pagans represented the Sun-God, *viz.*, as standing by the Tree of Life and holding a round object meant for the phallic apple, has not yet been dealt with in any way.

It is however desirable that before discussing the matter further we should ascertain the nature of the evidence, regarding this and kindred subjects, derivable from the coins of the Roman Empire.

CHAPTER X.

BEARING in mind the matters mentioned in the two last chapters, let us now pass in review the coins struck by the Romans, and make a note of such features as may, directly or indirectly, bear upon the history of the cross.

The first cross we meet with on the coins in question, is upon one of Julius Cæsar; who was appointed *Flamen Dialis* B.C. 87, *Pontiff* B.C. 74, Military Tribune B.C. 73, Quæstor B.C. 68, *Pontifex Maximus* B.C. 63, and Dictator B.C. 49.

The cross in question consists of the name *C. Cossutius Maridianus* arranged as a cross of four equal arms. And it should be noted that it is admitted, even by such well-known authorities as Mr. C. W. King, M.A., that the name was so arranged out of compliment to the official in question *because his name had reference to the meridian sun.*[1]

Upon a coin struck by Cæsar's heir, the almost equally famous Augustus (Consul B.C. 43, Emperor B.C. 29—A.C. 14), about twenty years before our era, we see a head of the Sun-God Bacchus upon one side ; and on the reverse a man presenting a military standard, the banner of which is ornamented with a St. Andrew's cross.

Two other coins of the same reign and about the same date, have upon them representations of military standards bearing the same symbol.

Upon another coin struck by Augustus we see a crescent with a star or radiate sun within its horns, the ancient phallic symbol adopted by the followers of the prophet Muhammad centuries later.

A similar symbol occurs upon the coins of Hadrian (A.C. 117—138).

Upon two coins of Antoninus Pius (A.C. 138—161) we see the Sun-God Hercules plucking the Golden Apple from a tree around which the traditional serpent is coiled.

[1] *Early Christian Numismatics.*

On another coin of the same reign the Sun-God Hercules can be seen holding a round object which admittedly represents the Golden Apple; that symbol both of the Sun-God as (1) the bi-sexual Giver of Life and (2) the per sonification of the Male Principle, and of the Goddess who represented (1) the Love of the two sexes and (2) the Female Principle.

Upon another coin Jove holds a similar looking object.

Many coins issued in the name of Annia Galeria Faustina the wife of Antoninus Pius, and by Marcus Aurelius (A.C. 161—180), and in the name of his wife Annia Faustina, have upon them representations of Venus the Goddess of Love holding a round object which is admittedly meant for the Golden Apple. The favourite legends are *Venus Victrix*, *Venus Felix*, and *Venus Genetrix*, and of phallic import; and in one instance the Goddess of Love holds an infant wrapped in swaddling clothes as well as the phallic apple.

Other coins of Marcus Aurelius or his wife have upon them representations of Eternity as a female figure holding a round object. In some cases the round object is surmounted by a Phœnix.

Upon a coin struck by Lucius Aurelius Verus (A.C. 160-169) that ruler is to be seen holding a round object surmounted by a Victory.

On the coins of Commodus (A.C. 180—192) sometimes Jove and sometimes the Emperor holds a small round object. A Victory in some cases surmounts it.

Venus holding the Golden Apple—that is, a round object which in such instances is admitted to have represented the Golden Apple—is to be seen upon many coins issued in the name of Lucilla, the sister of Commodus.

Upon coins issued by Caius Pescennius Niger a small round object surmounted by a Victory is to be seen in the hand of Jove.

On a coin struck by Septimus Severus (A.C. 193—211) we see Rome represented as a female figure with a shield at her side marked with a cross.

Upon another coin we see the Goddess of Love holding a round object admittedly meant for the Golden Apple, while a child is stationed at her feet. The legend is *Venus Genetrix.*

Among the coins issued in the name of Julia Domna, the wife of the last named Emperor, are nearly a dozen varieties upon which Venus is represented as holding a round object. A crescent occurs upon the reverse in some instances.

Upon several coins of Caracalla (A.C. 211—217) we see that Emperor holding a small round object surmounted by a Victory; upon others he is to be seen holding a Victory only.

Various coins issued in the name of Fulvia Plantilla the wife of Caracalla, show us the Goddess of Love holding a round object. **The** legends are *Venus Felix* and *Venus Victrix.*

In the reign of Elagabalus or Heliogabalus (A.C. 218—222) a coin was struck on which we see the Goddess Astarte, Ashtoreth, Ishtar, or Venus, holding a cross.

Venus holding a round object is to be seen upon many coins issued in the names of Soæmias the mother of Elagabalus, his wife Julia Aquilia Severa, Julia Mammæa the mother of Alexander Severus, and his wife Orbiana.

On a coin of the Emperor Decius (A.C. 249—251) struck at Mæonia, we meet with the so-called "Monogram of Christ" upon a Roman coin in the form ☒ for the first time.

Upon a coin of Trebonianus Gallus (A.C. 251—

254) Eternity is represented as a female holding a small round object.

On another coin of this reign we see a Phœnix instead of a Victory upon the round object held by the Emperor.

Many of the coins of ancient Rome acclaim the Sun-God as the Saviour, and upon a coin issued by Gallienus (A.C. 254—268) we see the Sun-God Apollo holding a cross.

Upon a coin issued by the younger Valerian we see the Sun-God holding a small round object.

A coin struck by Tetricus (A.C. 267—264) has upon its reverse a representation of the Sun-God holding a round object, while in the field near the Sun-God is a cross.

On a coin issued by Claudius II. we see the Sun-God Hercules holding a round object admittedly meant for the Golden Apple.

Upon a coin issued by Aurelianus we see the Sun-God holding a round object surmounted by a crescent.

On a coin issued by Vabalathus we see the Sun-God Hercules holding a round object admittedly representing the Golden Apple.

Upon a coin of Numerianus (A.C. 283—284) we see the Goddess of Love holding a round object surmounted by a Victory. Such instances as this should be specially noted, as nothing distinguishes the round objects so surmounted from those held by Venus which admittedly represent the Golden Apple, and the present fashion of our symbol the Coronation Orb or Imperial Apple is due to the fact that a century later Theodosius II. Emperor of Constantinople started the idea of substituting a cross for the Victory.

Upon several coins of Carinus (A.C. 282—284) we see the Sun-God holding a small round object.

On other coins of this reign Eternity appears as a female holding a small round object surmounted by a Phœnix.

Upon the coins issued in the name of Magnia Urbica, wife of Carinus, on which we see Venus holding a small round object which admittedly represented the Golden Apple, the Crescent frequently accompanies the representations of the Goddess of Love.

On coins issued by Diocletian (A.C. 284—305) we see both Jove and the Sun-God holding a small round object ; like the Emperor himself. A Victory in some cases surmounts it.

The Sun-God Hercules holding a round object which admittedly signified the Golden Apple is to be seen on other coins issued during this reign.

Among the coins issued by Diocletian's co-Emperor Maximian, is one bearing a representation of the Sun-God Hercules in the Garden of the Hesperides near the Tree encircled by the Serpent he slew. The Sun-God holds a round object representing a Golden Apple plucked from the Tree in question.

On the reverse of another coin bearing the names both of Jove the All-Father and Hercules the Sun-God, we see the latter represented as holding a round object, admittedly meant for the Golden Apple.

In some cases where Hercules holds the Golden Apple—for instance, upon a coin bearing the legend *Herculi invicto Aug.*—the Golden Apple is surmounted by a Victory.

A coin issued by Constantius Chlorus, the ruler of Gaul and father of Constantine the Great, represents the Sun-God Hercules in the act of plucking a Golden Apple from the famous Tree.

A coin issued in the joint names of Galerius

and Constantius Chlorus, bearing the legend *Genio Populi Romani,* has in the field on the reverse side a cross, which takes the place occupied upon otherwise similar coins by a star-like object not improbably representing the sun.

Such are the more striking features of the evidence which can be obtained from the Roman coins issued prior to the accession of Constantine to the throne of Gaul.

The reader will have seen that the symbol of the cross occurs several times upon the coins in question, and in almost if not quite every instance in connection with the Sun-God.

The fact that upon a coin of Julius Cæsar, and therefore before our era, a cross admittedly occurs as a symbol of the sun, will also have been remarked.

It will also have been noticed in how very large a number of cases the round symbol which was a precursor of our Coronation Orb admittedly signified the Golden Apple, and therefore was of phallic import.

Another point which the reader cannot very well fail to bear in mind, is that where the Goddess of Love, as the representative of the sex whose felicity lies in motherhood or the

victorious production of life, is seen carrying the
symbol in question, the surrounding legend is
Venus *Genetrix*, or *Victrix*, or *Felix*, or some
variation or other of the same ; and that the said
legends are obviously phallic in signification.

If we also keep before us the fact that the
Golden Apple whether held by the Sun-God or
his complement the Goddess of Love, was at
times surmounted by the figure of Victory for
which Christian Emperors gradually and only
gradually substituted the figure of the cross, it
is curious to note that in early Christian representations of the Christ he is often to be seen
with the Apple or forbidden fruit of the Tree of
Life or of the knowledge of good and evil.

When the Christ is in such cases depicted as a
youth, the phallic apple is usually to be seen
lying near him ; but when the Christ is represented as a man, it is placed in his hand.

For instance a good example of the Christ
holding the fruit of the Tree of Life is reproduced for us in the well known work on the
likeness of Jesus by the late Thomas Heaphy. [1]
Here we see, in a picture which occurs upon a

---

[1] *The Likeness of Christ*, p. 20.

glass ornament found in the Catacombs of Rome in the tomb of a Christian named Eutychia, an illustration of the Christ standing by the side of the Tree of Life. The rays of the Sun surround the head of the Christ, and in his hand is the phallic Apple.

It will have been remarked that the round object to be seen upon innumerable Roman coins in the hand of this or that ruler or deity, and popularly supposed to have always represented the round world upon which we dwell although it is at the same time believed that the world was not then considered to be round, frequently occurs in the hand of a female figure representing Eternity. It is self-evident that a representation of the world we live on is less likely to have been so placed than a symbol of Life.

A still more striking fact, which cannot fail to have been noticed by the reader of the evidence from the coins of ancient Rome quoted in the earlier part of this chapter, is that in several instances a Phœnix and not a Victory surmounts the so-called orb. For the story of the Phœnix was derived from the Egyptian City of the Sun. [1] And the fabulous bird in question was,

---

[1] Herodotus II., 73.

according to Tacitus as well as Herodotus, specially connected with the temple of the Sun-God at Heliopolis.

Upon this point it may be added that the famous story of the Phœnix seems to have been known to the writer of *Job;* the Septuagint version of *Job* xxix. 18, being " I shall die in my nest and shall multiply my days as the Phœnix" according to some of the best authorities.

The various ages allotted to this allegorical bird had reference to the calendar ; as indeed we learn from Pliny, who tells us that

"The revolution of the Great Year in which the seasons and stars return to their former places, agrees with the life of this bird."[1]

This is borne out by the periods spoken of as the lifetime of the Phœnix ; as among them are one of 600 years, the Great Year referred to by Josephus and others, and one of 1,461 years, which was the Sothic period of the Egyptians.

It is also clear that, like the .Victory and the Golden Apple it surmounted, the Phœnix and its wonderful egg were not only connected with the Sun-God, but also had a phallic signification.

[1] Pliny, x., 2.   [2] Tacitus, *Annal.* vi., 28.

The problem as to whether bird or egg first existed scarcely applies to the fabulous Phœnix and its equally fabulous egg, and need not be discussed here. Suffice it to say that the round object from which that Christian symbol the Coronation Orb is descended, though it may at times have more or less represented the world upon which we dwell, seems to have primarily signified, as associatèd with each other in idea, both the Golden Apple of Love and the Phœnix-like life principle enshrined in the Egg, both the egg-like *Cosmos* or Universe and Eternity ; but in all, and through all, and above all, the basis of all power whether finite or infinite, *viz.*, Life.

It is therefore not surprising to find that the monarchs of ancient days claimed to rule by divine right as vice-gerents of the Sun-God, to whose favouring influence all earthly life is traceable ; and caused themselves to be represented, upon Roman coins as receiving the Golden Apple, and upon Egyptian monuments as receiving the Cross, from the Sun-God, as the symbol of their authority.

Yet another point to be borne in mind, is that we Christians are expressly taught that God the Father and God the Son are as nearly identical as the ancients considered the Central Fire, which they deemed the Parent of all things, and the Warmth and Light issuing therefrom to be ; or the Sun's disc and the emanations therefrom ; the Christ being represented as saying " I and My Father are one " and " He that hath seen Me hath seen the Father." For though we describe ours as a *co-equal* Trinity, no such identity with either God the Father or God the Son is affirmed of God the Holy Ghost, and it is remarkable that in our ancient illustrations of the Three Persons, both the First and the Second are represented as holding the so-called globe and Cross, while the Third, even where depicted as of human shape like the other two, is not.

The fact is that the co-equality of the Holy Spirit of a God who is Himself, as Jesus declared, a Spirit, is an idea which did not find much acceptance among Christians till a comparatively late date and is the outcome of confused thought. And the separate personality of this Spirit of a Spirit being entirely a Christian conception, and without a counterpart in the theology of the ancients, few if any Pagan symbols such as the so-called globe and the cross would have been associated with it in any case.

CHAPTER XI.

WE are more or less in the habit of
assuming that just as Paul, the founder
of the catholic faith, was converted, not altogether
by reason but as it were by force and with the
rapidity of a flash of lightning, under the rays
of a meridian sun (" About *noon* suddenly there
shone from heaven a great light round about
me," *Acts* xxii. 6 ; " At *mid-day*," *Acts* xxvi. 13),
so Constantine, the establisher of that faith as
the State Religion of the empire in which Paul
was so proud of his rights as a citizen, was in
similarly rapid fashion converted by the appearance of a miraculous " cross " of light and an
accompanying legend above a meridian sun
(" At *mid-day*," Eusebius, *Vit. Const. I.*).

But, as has already been pointed out, this
alleged vision of Constantine is said to have

taken place during his march upon Rome in the year A.C. 312; and during the remaining twenty-five years of his life he acted rather as if he were converting Christianity into what he thought most likely to be accepted by his subjects as a catholic religion, than as if he had been converted to the teachings of Jesus the Nazarene.

The fact is that Constantine was favourable to our religion out of policy rather than conviction; and if after refusing so long he did indeed, a quarter of a century after the alleged vision, consent to be baptised when ill and dying, policy doubtless swayed him even then.

Anyway, as has already been stated and will now be seen, the evidence of his coins conclusively shows that the God to whom Constantine from first to last attributed his victories, was—the Sun-God.

Upon one coin issued by Constantine we see upon the reverse a nude figure crowned with rays, with the right hand elevated toward the east, and a round object in the left hand. In the field is a cross widened at the extremities, and the surrounding legend is a significant one, *Soli Invicto Comiti.* This coin was struck years after the alleged conversion of Constantine, and the combined reference to the Sun-God and use of the cross are worthy of special notice.

Upon two somewhat similar coins of Constantine the cross is placed within a circular wreath of bay or laurel.

On another coin with the same legend we see the same nude figure crowned with rays, representing the Sun-God and carrying a round object; while in the field we see the Gaulish symbol, sometimes called a cross, which by the addition of a loop was, as we shall see later on, turned into the so-called Monogram of Christ.

Upon a coin with the anything but Christian legend *Marti Conservatori,* is a cross with four equal arms.

On a somewhat similar coin with the same legend, the helmet on the reverse is ornamented with the so-called Monogram of Christ.

Upon another coin we see Mars leaning on a shield adorned with the so-called Monogram of Christ, the legend being *Marti Patri Conservatori.*

On a coin issued in the name of his son Crispus during the reign of Constantine, we see two Victories holding a shield upon a pedestal marked with a cross of four equal arms.

A similar cross appears upon a coin issued during this reign in the name of another son of Constantine.

Upon a coin bearing the inscription *Constantinus Max. Aug.* we see upon the reverse a cross of four equal arms.

On an otherwise similar coin a compound *tau* cross of four equal arms, ✠, appears.

Upon a well-known engraving of a coin in the *Annales Ecclesiastici* of Baronius, the ☧ form of the so-called Monogram of Christ appears upon the helmet of Constantine. Some authorities, however, state that this is copied as the familiar ☧ in error; what appeared on the helmet being the Gaulish symbol ✳ with a dot representing a star near the top of the vertical bar. Such a dot can be seen in a similar place upon two or three coins bearing the legend *Virtus Exercit.*

On another coin the legend *Gloria Exercitus* surrounds two soldiers holding military standards, between which is the symbol of the cross.

On a somewhat similar coin the compound *tau* cross, of which we have already noted an example, occurs between the standards.

A cross of four equal arms appears upon a coin bearing the legend *Pax Publica.*

A coin issued during the reign of Constantine the Great in the name of his son Constantine, has upon its reverse a cross of four equal arms, the extremities of which are rounded.

On an otherwise similar coin the compound tau cross appears.

Upon a coin bearing the inscription *Constantinus Max. Aug.* a cross of four equal arms occurs near a soldier armed with spear and shield.

On the reverse of one coin we see two soldiers holding military standards, and between the standards the so-called Monogram of Christ appears.

A coin of similar type was issued during the reign of Constantine the Great in the name of his son Constantine.

Upon a coin which on the obverse bears the inscription *Constantinus Max. Aug.*, we see upon the reverse Victory carrying a palm. In the field is the symbol ⚷. The surrounding motto is *Victoria Constantini Aug.*

Several coins with the legend *Gloria Exercitus* have upon the same side two soldiers with a labarum or military standard between them, upon the banner of which is the symbol ⚲.

On a coin with the legend *Victoria Cæsar NN* we see Victory carrying a palm. In the field is the Gaulish symbol ✳.

The reverse of another coin has the legend *Constantinus Aug.*, and represents Constantine as holding a labarum or military standard terminating in a round object. Upon the banner is the symbol ⚲.

On a coin bearing upon its obverse the inscription *Constantinopolis*, we see upon the other side a figure of Victory and a cross of four equal arms.

On another coin bearing the same legend we see upon the reverse Victory standing upon a ship, and to the left the so-called monogram.

Upon another coin we see the same symbol above the wolf and twins of the city of Rome.

A rare coin bears upon the obverse the inscription *Constantinus Max. Aug.*, and on the reverse, surrounded by the legend *Spes Publica*, a labarum or military standard the handle or base of which transfixes a serpent. Upon the banner three globules are embroidered, and the symbol ☧ appears above the cross-bar from which the banner hangs.

Upon one medal or coin of Constantine we see the significant legend *Soli Invicto Aeterno Aug.* inscribed around the quadriga of the Sun God Phœbus.

On another piece struck by Constantine the Great, the Sun-God is given the title *Comes Aug. ;* Companion, Guardian, or Saviour, of the Emperor.

Upon several coins we see the legend *Comiti Aug. NN*, and, surrounded by the same, the Sun-God holding a small round object.

On numerous other coins also, the Sun-God is represented as holding a small round object.

Other significant Sun-God legends to be met upon the coins of this alleged Christian Emperor, are *Comis Constantini Aug., Soli Invicto, Soli Comiti Augg. NN, Soli Invicto Com. D.N. ;* and the like.

Upon a coin bearing the legend *Soli Comiti Aug. N.* we see the Sun-God presenting Constantine with a small round object surmounted by a Victory.

On a coin with the legend *Pax Augustorum,*

Constantine holds a standard ornamented with a cross.

Upon another coin Constantine is to be seen holding what is said to be a representation of the Zodiac.

On a coin issued in his own name, as upon others already mentioned as issued in the names of his sons, we see two Victories supporting a shield upon an altar ornamented with a cross.

Upon a somewhat similar coin the altar is ornamented with the star-like object which in days of old so often stood for the radiate sun.

A coin with the inscription *Divo Constantino*, and on the reverse the legend *Aeterna Pietas* and a representation of Constantine holding a round object surmounted by the symbol ⳨, though usually included in the coins of that Emperor was evidently struck after his death and deification.

The same remark applies to a somewhat similar coin, which has an additional symbol in a plain cross in the field to the right of the Emperor-God.

It should be noted that the question here arises as to how far it is fair of us to claim this cross and so-called Monogram of Christ as

Christian and at the same time denounce as Pagan the deification of Constantine referred to upon the same coins.

As to the coins of Constantine the Great as a whole, it need only be remarked once more that while upon many of the pieces struck by him Constantine attributed his victories to the Sun-God, not upon a single one of them did he attribute them to the Christ; while it was ever the Sun-God and never the Christ whom he alluded to on his coins as his Companion, Partner, Guardian, or Saviour.

This being so, how can we honestly claim that the so-called Monogram of Christ, and other forms of the cross, were ever placed upon his coins by Constantine as symbols of the Christ, yet never as symbols of the Sun-God?

CHAPTER XII.

PASSING on to the Christian successors of Constantine the Great, we are at once met with the significant fact that Constantine the Second issued many different coins bearing a representation of the Sun-God holding a small round object; and, as the surrounding legend, *Claritas Reipublicae.*

Another coin of this son of Constantine the Great, and one which deserves special attention, has upon its reverse a Cross and a Crescent in juxtaposition, as if the cross signified the sun.

A very similar coin has the symbol ✳ between the military standards.

Upon another coin we see on the reverse both this Christian Emperor and the Sun-God; the former holding a small round object, and the latter crowning him. The surrounding legend is *Soli Invicto Comiti.*

The reverse of another coin bears the same Sun-God legend, and represents the Sun-God as holding a small round object.

Upon another coin we see Constantine holding a small round object surmounted by a Victory. On the reverse is the symbol ☧.

Constans I., another son of Constantine the Great, issued a coin on which he is represented as holding in one hand a simply formed labarum or military standard consisting of a straight pole terminating at the top in a cross-bar, from which hangs a banner bearing the symbol ☧ ; while in the other hand he holds a small round object surmounted by a *Phœnix.*

Constantius II., yet another son of Constantine the Great, issued a coin on which is the symbol ☧ between the letters A and Ω (? ΑΡΧΩ) ; the legend being *Salus Aug. Nostri.*

On another coin is Constantius II. as the Sun, upon one side ; and upon the other the symbol ☧ between the letters alpha and omega once again.

Nepotianus, a nephew of Constantine the

Great who took Rome in A.C. 350 but was killed as an usurper the same year, issued a coin on the reverse of which, surrounded by the legend *Urbs Roma*, is a female figure representing Rome and holding in her hand a round object surmounted by the symbol ✣.

The symbol ⳨ frequently occurs upon the coins of Valeus (A.C. 364-378). And upon one coin of this Emperor we see the letter P surmounting a cross; surrounded by the legend *Gloria Romanorum*.

Upon a coin of Valentinianus II. we see Victory holding a round object surmounted by a cross, the legend being *Victoria Augustorum*.

On the coins of Theodosius I. (A.C. 378-395) we find representations of the Emperor holding a round object surmounted by a Phœnix, and of the Emperor holding a round object surmounted by a Victory; as also of Victory holding a round object surmounted by a cross.

This Emperor Theodosius I., better known as Theodosius the Great, after securing sole control of the Roman Empire brought about the final disruption of the world-wide dominions of Rome by bequeathing them in two portions to his sons Arcadius and Honorius; the elder, Arcadius, becoming Emperor of Constantinople and the East, while the younger, Honorius, became Emperor of Rome and the West: A.C. 395.

Less than a century later, *viz.*, between the years A.C. 475 and 480, the Western Empire was finally extinguished by Odoacer; the Eastern Empire surviving it nearly a thousand years, lasting as the latter did from the partition in A.C. 395 to the capture of Constantinople by Mahomet II. in A.C. 1453.

It was, as stated in a previous chapter, upon the coins of an Emperor of the East, *viz.*, Theodosius II., that the first example occurs of a representation of an Emperor holding a round object surmounted by a cross; though, as has been noted, instances of Victory carrying an object so surmounted had previously occurred. And it need only be added that the symbols ✳ and ☧, often the centre of a circle or surrounded by a circular wreath of bay or laurel, continually occur upon the coins of the Eastern Empire, the symbol ✳ frequently, and the undisguised solar wheel, ⊕, upon the coins of Eudoxia, Theodosius II., Leo I., and others.

The evidence of the coins of the Roman Empire given in this and the two preceding chapters, coupled with the too-often forgotten fact that the only form of cross which could possibly be a representation of the instrument of execution to which Jesus was affixed was the very last form of cross to be adopted as a Christian symbol, cannot, it will be seen, lead the unprejudiced enquirer to any other conclusion than that the cross became the symbol of Christendom because the advent of Constantine and his Gauls made it a prominent symbol of the Roman Empire. And that the symbol in question was not altogether unconnected with Sun-God worship, should be equally clear to the reader.

CHAPTER XIII.

THE MONOGRAM OF CHRIST.

THE so-called "Monogram of Christ"—a term which has at one time or another been applied to each of the symbols ⊗ or ✳, ⊗ or ✷, and ⊕ or ⳨, as but variations of one and the same symbol—deserves a chapter to itself.

Though not first placed upon the coins of the Roman Empire by Constantine any more than was the right-angled cross of four equal arms or the so-called St. Andrew's cross, the symbol ✷ was, like the ✕ cross and the many varieties of right-angled crosses of four equal arms, first brought into prominence as a Roman symbol by the Emperor in question.

From the evidence at our disposal it would appear that Decius was the first Roman ruler

147

to make use of this form of the so-called Monogram of Christ. Anyhow, as has already been remarked, this symbol ☧ occurs upon a coin of the Emperor Decius struck at Mæonia about A.C. 250; and therefore more than half a century before the days of Constantine. And it is noteworthy that it was as a Pagan symbol that the ☧ thus first appeared upon the Roman coinage.

The coin in question is a bronze one, and the "Monogram of Christ" occurs in the centre of a Greek inscription surrounding a representation of the Sun-God Bacchus; and, apparently, as an amalgamation or contraction of the two Greek letters equivalent to our R and C H, *viz,:* the Greek letters P and X. [1]

Why these particular letters should have been contracted, is, however, uncertain; and the question arises as to whether the ☧ first arose as a contraction of such Greek letters, or as an amalgamation of the Roman letters P and X, or as the cross X *plus* the Greek P (our *R*) as the initial letter of the Greek name for Rome.

Moreover if it be decided that the symbol

---

[1] An engraving of the coin can be seen in Duruy's *Histoire des Romains*, Tom. vii.

first arose as a contraction of certain letters, yet further questions arise; *viz.* : in what order those letters were first read, and what word they first represented.

Before going into such matters as these, however, it is important that we should fully realise how certain it is that the so-called Monogram of Christ was originally a *Pagan* symbol. For even if this be not considered demonstrated by its occurrence upon a Roman coin long before, according to our Church, the Christ caused Constantine to use it as the military standard of the Gauls, it is clearly shown by its occurrence upon many relics of pre-Christian date.

The so-called " Monogram of Christ" can be seen, for instance, upon a monument of Isis, the Virgin Mother of the Sun-God, which dates from the second century before our era [1] Also upon the coins of Ptolemaeus ; on one of which is a head of Zeus Ammon upon one side, and an eagle bearing the ✸ in its claws upon the other. [2] The symbol in question also appears upon Greek money struck long before the birth of Jesus ; for instance upon certain varieties of

[1] Böckh, C.I.G. n. 4713 b.
[2] Berlin Collection 428.

the Attic tetradrachma.   And the ⚏ occurs upon many different coins of the first Herod, struck thirty years or more B.C.

Whether the Pagan ✳ and the Pagan ⚏ originally had the same signification or not, is uncertain.

Almost equally uncertain is the date at which we Christians first adopted these Pagan symbols as Christian symbols because they could be interpreted as formed of the two first letters of the Greek word ΧΡΙΣΤΟΣ, *Christos,* Christ.

The probability is that Christians had at least drawn attention to this possible interpretation of the symbols in question before the days of Constantine.   But this scarcely renders less noteworthy the fact, shown further on, that the favourite symbol of the Gaulish warriors, the solar wheel ⊛ or ⊕, was sooner or later altered by their leader into ⊛ or ⊕ to please the Christians ; while the symbols ✳ and ⚏ were also made use of by Constantine.

Which form of solar wheel, monogram, or cross, was that actually carried by the Gauls in triumph within the walls of Rome and set up by their leader in the heart of the Eternal City, is not quite certain.   But it is clear that as both the ✳ and the ⳾ appeared upon coins struck before our era, Constantine cannot very well have been ignorant of the fact that these were originally Pagan symbols, when he favoured the addition of a loop to the top of the vertical bar of the Gaulish solar symbols ⊛ or ✳ and ⊕ or ✚ in order that what his Gaulish army venerated as triumphal tokens might be accepted as symbols of victory by his Christian supporters also.

That this Gaulish monarch did so alter, and for the reason named, the symbol or symbols venerated by his troops, is admitted by, amongst others, that well known writer the Reverend S. Baring Gould, M.A. For, referring to the solar wheel as a symbol of the Sun-God venerated by the ancient Gauls, this author tells us that Constantine

"Adopted and adapted the sign for his standards, and the *Labarum* of Constantine became a common Christian symbol. That there was policy in his conduct we can hardly doubt; the symbol he set up gratified the Christians in his army on one side and the Gauls on the other. For the former it was a sign compounded of the initial letters of Christ, to the latter it was the token of the favour of the solar deity."[1]

---

[1] *Strange Survivals*, 286.

As the fact that both the ⚹ and ⳨ were in use as symbols before the commencement of our era thoroughly disposes of our contention as Christians that the so-called " Monogram of Christ " had its origin in the formation of a monogram out of the two first letters of the Greek word ΧΡΙΣΤΟΣ (*Christos*, Christ), it is clear that these symbols must have had some other origin.

Assuming that the symbols ⚹ and ⳨ had the same origin, and the same signification, and that if the ⳨ was a combination of two letters the Greek or Latin T (instead of X) was not one of them ; or rather, as these would be very considerable assumptions, more or less confining our attention to the ⚹ as the more likely of the two to have arisen as a combination of the Greek letters P and X ; let us in passing briefly enquire into the origin of the so-called Monogram of Christ as a Pagan symbol.

If we seek for that origin as a combination of the first two letters of some other Greek word than Christos, *Christ*, and for the moment assume the letters P and X to have occurred in the same order as in that word, we see at once that the monogram may have been derived either from the word Chrestos, *Good*, or the word Chronos, *Time*, or the word Chrusos, *Gold*.

There is, by the way, another curious connection between the three Greek words in question. For the name of the famous god Kronos or Cronos was often spelt ΧΡΟΝΟΣ, *i.e.*, Chronos. [1] And this god Chronos—the father of Zeus; and more or less a personification of Time, the Old Father from whom we are all descended—was identical with Saturn, while the Saturnian Age was, as in Virgil's fourth eclogue, ever that spoken of as the Golden age when the ancients were referring to what they pictured as the good old times.

It will not do, however, to assume that if the symbol we are considering first arose as a combination of the Greek letters P and X, they were of necessity taken from, and representative of, a word in which they occur in the same order as in *Christos*. And the fact that in the ☧, if not also in the ✳, the P is the leading feature, gives emphasis to the point in question.

If we suppose that the so-called monogram

---

[1] *e.g.*, Arist. *Mundi.*

arose as a combination of the Greek letters in question occurring in the order **P X**, the student of such matters can scarcely fail to note that the letters in question occur in that order as the centre both of the word **APXH**, the *Head, Chief,* or *First;* and also as the centre of the kindred word **APXΩ**, *to be first,* the only remaining letters of which, and therefore the first and the last of this word as of the old Greek alphabet, are, as will be seen, Alpha and Omega, the letters so continually placed on either side of the symbol ☧ in Christian times.

In this connection it should be pointed out that according to some of the best authorities the first ☧ which occurs upon any Roman coin, coming as it does after the letter *alpha* in a Greek inscription, should be taken with that letter as forming the **PX** of **APX**, the latter being an abbreviation of some form or other of the title *Archon.* This title was that given to the dignitary who was at one and the same time the chief magistrate of the state and its chief priest, and it may be worth remark that as Bacchus was the deity worshipped in Lydia, the Archon in question would therefore have been the chief priest of the Sun-God.

Several writers have, in their zeal for our religion, outrun their discretion, and gone so far as to assume that the existence of the so-called monogram of Christ upon this coin of the Emperor Decius is due to some Christian having been employed in turning out the coin in question, and having in *his* zeal surreptitiously introduced a symbol of his faith. But though gravely supported by more than one great authority, this is obviously an absurd position to take up. And in any case the facts remain that it was in this instance placed over a representation of the Sun-God, and had for centuries been in use as a Pagan symbol.

Passing on, however, we have next to note that, as before hinted, even if the symbol ⚹ arose as a combination of two letters, though we know that symbol to have been often used as a contraction of the Greek letters P and X (our R and CH), there is no proof that it arose as a combination of two Greek letters; and the symbol may have arisen as a combination of the Roman letters P and X.

It should therefore be pointed out that in the inscriptions which have come down to us from the Gaulish Christians of the sixth, seventh, and

eighth centuries after Christ, the symbols ✳
and ⚵ are continually used as contractions of
the Latin word PAX, *Peace*. For though the
fact that the Monogram was often so interpreted
by Christians centuries A.C. can by no means
be considered evidence that it was thus that
it first arose as a Pagan symbol centuries B.C.
such a possibility should be kept before us.

But did the so-called Monogram of Christ
first come into being as a combination of two
letters; Greek, Roman, or otherwise?

Even this is not certain, for this pre-Christian
symbol may originally have been a cross, as a
symbol of Life and of the Sun-God, *plus* the
Greek letter P as the initial character of the
word "Rome" in what may be called the court
language of the time.

Such an explanation would more or less
account for the variations ✳ and ⚵ ; these
being obviously the natural ways of adding the
letter P, signifying Rome, to the crosses ✕ and
✚ respectively.

All the foregoing references to the origin of
the so-called monogram as a Pagan symbol of
pre-Christian date, are but speculations however.
Its origin cannot be ascertained for certain.

The revival of this pre-Christian symbol, and the prominence given to it upon the coins of the Roman Empire, *are*, however, traceable. And, as has been shown, they are traceable to Constantine; who induced the Christians to accept as the Monogram of the Christ, and therefore as a Christian as well as a Gaulish symbol of victory, the Solar Wheel venerated by the Gaulish conquerors of Rome.

Nowadays the so-called Monogram of Christ is almost always reproduced for us as ✳ or ✝ ; but the fact that Constantine sometimes so used it should not blind us to the facts that it was at first usually the centre of a circle, like the spokes of a wheel; and that the undisguised solar wheel ⊛ appears upon not a few of the coins issued by the Christian successors of Constantine, while since his reign the solar wheel ⊕ and many an artistic variation of the same have been Christian symbols, and when in our ornamentation of ecclesiastical properties we omit the circle we as often as not make the cross itself wheel-like by rounding the extremities and widening them till they nearly meet.

Moreover it should not be forgotten that it

was evidently one form or other of the solar wheel of the Gauls, *plus* the politic loop to one of its spokes, which Constantine and his Gaulish warriors are said to have seen above the meridian sun, with the divinely written legend **ΕΝ ΤΟΥΤΩ ΝΙΚΑ**, *By this conquer*, attached. For though that miraculous symbol is referred to as a "cross," the Monogram itself was so referred to; and Eusebius, after telling us that the Christ appeared to Constantine and commanded him to make a military standard for the Sun-God worshipping Gauls, "With the same sign which he had seen in the heavens," expressly describes this as composed of "Two letters indicating the name of the Christ, the letter P being intersected with X at the centre." And on this particular Labarum of Constantine, as on the majority of the Labara represented upon his coins, the ☧ was the centre of a circle or circular wreath, like the spokes of a wheel.[1]

In any case the fact that the symbol ☧ was a Pagan one centuries before the Christ is said to have made it a Christian one for the Sun-God

---

[1] Bar. *Ann.* A.C. 312.

worshipping Gauls to follow on to victory, coupled with the facts that they are said to have seen it above the mid-day sun, and that it was admittedly a politic adaptation of the Solar Wheel, show us how much Eusebius and other Christian chroniclers both invented and suppressed, and also how largely the influence of Sun-God worship permeated and moulded our religion.

In this connection it may be noted, as a curious fact rather than as evidence, that according to some authorities the so-called Mono grams of Christ were in earlier ages Monograms of the Sun-God Osiris. [1] Also that both Socrates and Sozomen tell us that when the temple of the Sun-God Serapis at Alexandria was pulled down, the symbol of the Christ was discovered upon its foundations and the Christians made many converts in consequence : a somewhat significant statement.

Moreover we are told that upon every *Dies Solis,* or in other words upon that day of the week which throughout the Roman Empire was held sacred to the Sun-God and throughout

[1] Basnage, iii., 23.

Christendom is called Sun-day, Constantine
made his troops, assembled under what was
admittedly a solar symbol, recite at a given time,
which was probably dawn or mid-day, a prayer
commencing "We acknowledge thee to be God
alone, and own that our victories are due to
thy favour."[1]   Who could this God have been
but the Sun-God, seeing that it was to the
Sun-God that Constantine upon his coins ever
attributed his victories?   And what is more
likely than that, wishing to take a friendly view
of the deity worshipped by their supporters the
Christians, it was as conceiving the Christ to be
but the latest addition to the many conceptions
of the Sun-God, that Constantine altered the
solar symbols of his troops into the so-called
Monograms of Christ, and that his troops
accepted the alterations?

And, passing from the symbol to the deity
represented, let us remember that it is recorded
that various Christian paintings of ancient times
bore upon them the dedicatory words *DEO
SOLI*. For this remarkable legend means both
" To God alone" and " To the Sun-God," both

---

[1] Eusebius, *Vit. Const.* iv.

" To the Sole God " and " To the God Sol ; "
and forcibly reminds us, not only of the
prayer which Constantine caused his troops to
repeat, but also of that fine address to the
" universally adored " Sun-God commencing

> " Latium calls thee Sol because in honour thou
>   art Solitary,
>   After the Father." [1]

Now, as will be shown further on a cross of
some description or other was in every land
accepted as the symbol of the universally
adored Sun-God.   And while not a single
one of the many books forming the New
Testament states that Jesus was executed upon
a cross-shaped instrument, and the *first* crosses
Christians used as signs or symbols bore every
form but that which a cross-shaped instrument
of execution would have borne, the Christians
of the fourth century, as we have seen, went
out of their way to claim even the so-called
Monogram of Christ as a cross ; Eusebius so
carefully speaking of it as such even where he
relates that Constantine and his soldiers saw

---

[1] Martianus Capella.

it above the meridian sun, that one might not unreasonably imagine him to be claiming it as Christian because it was more or less cruciform and therefore more or less like the world-wide symbol of the Sun-God.

CHAPTER XIV.

THE CROSS OF THE LOGOS.

HAVING made clear the part played by Constantine in the prominence given in his lifetime to the cross as a symbol of the Roman Empire and therefore of what he made its State Religion, and having also shown that while the Christian chroniclers of those days are silent concerning the various forms of crosses placed by Constantine upon his coins they went out of their way to allude to the so-called Monogram of Christ as a cross, to claim it as such, and even to associate it with the sun, let us now turn our attention again to the pre-Christian cross.

So great was the veneration in which that phallic and solar symbol the cross was held in the ages which preceded the birth and death of Jesus, that the philosophers of those days even went so far as to declare that the cross was the figure of the Life or Soul of the Universe.

Though it is a matter of very considerable importance, we Christians for some reason or other ignore the fact that long before our era commenced philosophers thus conceived the figure of the cross to be the symbol of the *Logos* of God.

Now although, following the Gospel of St. John, we have made it a main article of our belief that the Logos, really the Thought *plus* Speech, of God, became about the year B.C. 4 specially incarnate in the person of Jesus the Nazarene, we ought not to forget that, being the one Power by which all that ever came into existence was created and all that exists is sustained, the Logos in any case ever was, is, and will be, incarnate in every sentient being.

As the Logos of God (or, as the Authorised Version of the Bible into English most inadequately renders it in the first chapter of St. John's Gospel, the *Word* of God) was by the philosophers called the " Intellectual Sun " and the " Light of the World ", [1] being, as a personification of the *Thought* and *Speech* of the

---

[1] *e.g.* Philo, *De Somniis,* i.

All-Father, a personification of Wisdom and Reason (which, in an even more real sense than the emanations of the physical sun, form the " Light of the World," or, as the original text of the New Testament puts it, the " Light of the *Cosmos* "), the fact that pre-Christian philosophers affirmed that the cross was the symbol of the said " Light of the Cosmos," is obviously one which every writer concerning the cross as a Christian symbol ought in common honesty to deal with.

That pre-Christian philosophers did so affirm, can be seen by turning to the *Timæus* of Plato, where, referring to the begetting of the Universal Soul (whom Philo, another pre-Christian philosopher, speaks of as the " Second God "; and as God's " Beloved Son," " Image," " Ambassador," " Mediator," and " First-Begotten "), Plato says

" Such was the whole plan of the Eternal God about the God that was to be :—and in the centre he put the soul which he diffused throughout the body :—and he made the Universe a circle moving in a circle. Having these purposes in view he created the world a blessed God :—he made the soul on this wise—joined—at the centre like the letter X." [1]

---

[1] *Timæus*, 34–36.

Concerning this pronouncement of the great Teacher he so revered, Proclus wrote as follows

"Two circles will be formed, of which one is interior but the other is exterior. One of these is called the circle of the Same and one the circle of the Different, or of the Fixed and of the Variable, or rather of the Equinoctial Circle and of the Zodiac. The circle of the Different revolves about the Zodiac, but the circle of the Same about the Equinoctial. Hence we conceive that the right lines are not to be applied to each other at right angles but like the letter X, as Plato says, so as to cause the angles to be equal only at the summit but those on each side and the successive angles to be unequal. For the Equinoctial Circle does not cut the Zodiac at right angles. Such therefore in short is the mathematical discussion of the figure of the (Universal) Soul." [1]

Even the Fathers of the Christian Church admitted that their ideas of the Son of God and of the cross being his symbol, were more or less derived from pre-Christian philosophers. For we find Justin Martyr remarking that Plato declared that

"The Power next to the Supreme God was figured in the shape of the letter X upon the universe." [2]

And in another place this famous Father states that

"Whereas Plato, philosophising about the Son of God,

---

[1] *Theol. Plat.*   [2] *Apol.*

says God expressed him upon the universe in the shape of the letter X, he evidently took the hint from Moses, who took brass and made the sign of the cross and placed it by the holy tabernacle, and declared that if people would look upon that cross and believe they would be saved." [1]

The value of all this evidence is so obvious that its mere parade is almost sufficient.

It should however be pointed out that this cross X , being avowedly adopted by the pre-Christian philosophers as the symbol of the "Logos" or "First-begotten" of God in preference to the ╋ because the zodiac or pathway of the Sun does not "cross" the equator at right angles, was clearly a solar symbol. And it may be added that though Justin Martyr is careful to claim this particular solar cross as a symbol of the Christ, no one claims that Jesus was executed upon an instrument so shaped ; while the story that St. Andrew was affixed to an instrument of execution so shaped, is admittedly a worthless legend.

This claim of Justin Martyr that the solar cross of the philosophers was a pre-Christian

---

[1] *Apol.*

symbol of the Christ, is, when considered in connection with the fact that nearly all the Fathers allude to the figure of the cross, *any* kind of cross, as a life-giving symbol from time immemorial, significant of much.

CHAPTER XV.

THAT the symbol of the cross was widely venerated in Europe long before our era, is well known to archæologists.

Of Britain in those days we know next to nothing, history being almost silent upon the subject and relics conspicuous by their absence. The cross is however a conspicuous feature upon certain funeral urns which are said to date back to the period in question. And it is noteworthy that both it and the solar wheel occur upon several of the earliest British coins; which whether issued as some say before, or as others aver after, the advent of Julius Cæsar, were admittedly of pre-Christian date.

Evidences of the veneration of the cross in France before our era are so numerous and

easily ascertainable, that it will only be necessary
to refer the reader to the *Collection Roujou*, the
pages of the *Revue de Numismatique,* and the
writings of Messieurs De la Saussaye, Lenor-
mant, De Saulcy, E. Lambert, and other
French authorities.

If, continuing our journey eastwards, we pass
over the border into the northern provinces of
Italy, we find equally striking evidence of
the pre-Christian veneration of the symbol in
question.

Let us take for example the evidence fur-
nished by the remarkable discoveries made in the
pre-Christian cemetery unearthed at Gola-Secca.
For upon a very large proportion of the
articles discovered in the ancient tombs of the
cemetery in question, a cross of some kind is
the prominent feature.

Particulars of these articles can be found
recorded in the literary and scientific journals
of France. And the conclusion arrived at by
the authorities upon such matters cannot be
better put than in the revised edition in book
form of an article in the *Revue Archéologique*
by Monsieur G. de Mortillet.

After referring to the relics of so much of

ancient Gaul as is comprised in modern I
a subject he takes leave of in the words—

"But the pre-Christian cult of the cross was not confined to Savoy and the environs of Lyons. A glance at the coins of ancient Gaul is sufficient to show that it existed in nearly every part"

M. de Mortillet, crossing the frontier and dealing with the said tombs of Gola-Secca near Milan in Italy, sums up as follows

"One sees that there can be no doubt whatever concerning the use of the cross as a religious sign for a very long time before Christianity. The cult of the cross was well spread over Gaul before its conquest and already existed in Emilia in the Bronze Age, more than a thousand years before Jesus Christ."

Let us pass on to yet another country, Switzerland. Here also we find unexceptional evidence of the general recognition of the cross before our era as a symbol which should above all others be venerated.

The Lake Dwellings of Switzerland may be said to have been brought to light by the extraordinary drought experienced in the years A.C. 1853-4; for though piles and ancient remains were found upon the shores of various lakes before that date, no great heed was paid to them till the drought in question lowered the waters of the lake of Zurich and of other lakes to an unprecedented extent, and certain discoveries due thereto led to the matter being thoroughly investigated by antiquarians.

¯ The result was that many relics of the Lake Dwellers were found. And, placed upon those relics by this forgotten race of hoary antiquity as the sign they venerated, was the symbol of the cross.

These relics, preserved for us by the sediment carried into the lakes by various rivers, cannot be less than 3,000 years old, are not improbably 4,000 years old, and may quite possibly be 5,000 years old; some authorities—Monsieur Morlot for instance—estimating their age at from 6,000 to 7,000 years. Suffice it to record the fact that these relics are admittedly pre-Christian.

Upon the articles in question, as on those discovered in the pre-Christian tombs of Gola-Secca, the cross is stamped as a symbol of life, of good omen, and of salvation. Even dies for stamping articles with the cross have been dis-covered among the remains of the Lake Dwellers. And the crosses are of three kinds; (1) the right-angled cross of four equal arms, of which so many variations, some enclosed in circles and some with the extremities widened and rounded, are used as Christian symbols; (2) the other cross of four equal arms, known as the St. Andrew's cross or *Chi* cross; and (3) the Fylfot or Svastika cross.

The last named cross is a peculiar one of quite unmistakeable design; and there are two varieties, ⊔Ӻ and 卍, of which one is obviously an impression or reverse view of the other.

The names *Fylfot* and *Svastika* are very generally applied to both these symbols. The term *Svastika*, an Indian one, is however applied by the inhabitants of Hindostan to one only; they calling the other *Sauvastika*. And it is curious to note that the meanings attached to these names, though, like the symbols allied in nature, are, also like them, the reverse or negative or complement of each other.

For instance we are told by Sir G. Birdwood that the right handed Svastika signifies the Male Principle, the Sun on its daily journey from East to West, Light and Life; and that the left-handed Svastika signifies the Female Principle, the Sun in Hades or the Underworld on its

12

journey from West to East, Darkness and Death.[1]

This more or less official pronouncement may be taken as a fairly accurate one, although it is obvious that the annual as well as the diurnal movement of the Sun should have been referred to ; the half year between the Vernal Equinox and Autumnal Equinox representing Light and Life, and that between the Autumnal Equinox and Vernal Equinox Darkness and Death, just as clearly as do the half days between sunrise and sunset, sunset and sunrise. But it is to be feared that even those who remember how often Death and Darkness are referred to as periods of Gestation, will have some difficulty in seeing how a sign or symbol of the Female Power of Generation can have signified Death.

The fact of course is that the symbol in question represented both Life and Death, and represented the latter only in a minor sense and owing to the fact that the Female Principle of Life was regarded as the necessary reverse, negative, or complement of the Male Principle ;

---

[1] *Report on the Old Records of the India Office,* London, 1891, x., xi.

which latter, having of the two the better claim to be considered the starter of life, was the one more particularly identified with Life and therefore with the vernal Sun-God.

It would also appear that the two symbols in question to some extent signified Fire and Water; Fire being of course the Male Principle, Day, Summer, Light, and Life; and Water the Female Principle. This still further illustrates the point dealt with above; for though Water is the negative of Fire, yet Fire cannot produce Life without the aid of Water.

Returning however to our consideration of the cross as a symbol of Life of pre-Christian date and origin, and having already dealt with the lands now known as Britain, France, Italy, and Switzerland, let us now consider the evidence of Greece.

At Mycenæ and elsewhere Dr. Schliemann discovered, among other relics of a bygone age, not only articles marked with the Svastika cross and the cross of four equal arms, but even seals and dies giving impressions of such crosses; thus demonstrating how large and prominent a part the symbol of the cross played in pre-Christian times among those in whose classic

tongue the earliest known copies of the Christian
Scriptures were written centuries later.

It is also remarkable that Dr. Schliemann
found golden crosses in the previously unopened
tombs he discovered and explored at Mycenæ;
as many as five such crosses having in some
instances been placed with a single body by
those who sealed up the vaults in question
thousands of years ago and many centuries
before the commencement of our era.

As few if any unrifled tombs of so ancient a
date have been discovered in Greece and first
explored by a trustworthy investigator, and as,
moreover, it would only have been with the
bodies of important personages that crosses of
so valuable a material as gold would have been
buried, these discoveries, coupled with the self-
evident fact that crosses of more perishable
material may have been buried with the bodies
of less distinguished people, and by this time,
like both the bodies and the tombs which
enclosed them, have gone to dust, are most
remarkable. And they entirely corroborate the
testimony borne by the coins of ancient Gaul,
the contents of the tombs of Gola-Secca, and
the remains of the Lake Dwellers of Switzerland,

to the veneration paid long before our era by the inhabitants of Europe to the cross as the recognised symbol of Life. Nor as the symbol only of the life which ends in the grave, but also of the glorious hope that as the Sun, from whom we derive that life, whether considered from a daily or yearly point of view sinks but to rise again, even so we who owe our brief lives to the Sun-God, may, like the Giver of Life and only Saviour, rise from one life to another.

For whether the ancients were or were not unphilosophic enough to believe in the resurrection of bodies whose constituent atoms are continually changing and in time form part of other bodies, it is absurd to assume that they did not at times like ourselves conceive and dwell upon a hoped-for, if unexpected and improbable, Life-to-come.

Moreover it is with us, as it was with them, a *hope ;* and it is disingenuous to label as Christian what was pre-Christian, and to claim as ours what has been common to the reasoning minds of suffering men and women of all eras.

It is equally disingenuous on the part of us Christians to keep in the background the noteworthy fact that even in pre-Christian ages the symbol of that hope was—the cross.

CHAPTER XVI.

THE PRE-CHRISTIAN CROSS IN ASIA.

IF, leaving Europe, we pass on into Asia, we find that not only have the two varieties of Svastika crosses for thousands of years played a prominent part as a religious symbol in Hindostan, Thibet, and China, but that other kinds of crosses also were in bygone ages venerated by their inhabitants.

For instance our Eastern Empire is strewn with the remains of ancient temples built, like those of Christendom in later days, in the shape of a cross; and we are told that the oldest of its rock-hewn caves were planned after the same figure. It is also well-known that isolated stone crosses of pre-historic date are to be seen in various parts of India.

The evidence of Hindostan is however out-weighed by that obtainable from the antiquities of Western Asia, concerning some of which Sir A. H. Layard wrote:

178

"The crux ansata, the tau or sign of life, is found in the sculptures of Khorsabad, on the ivories of Nimroud—which as I have shown are of the same age—carried too by an Assyrian King." [1]

We have also to note the equally significant facts that the recognised symbol of the Phœnician Goddess of Love—Astarte, Ashtoreth, or Ishtar, the Bride of the Sun-God—was a cross; that a cross was also associated with the Phœnician Baal or Sun-God ; and that the circle and cross, now the symbol of the planet held sacred to the Goddess of Love, frequently occurs upon the ancient coins of Western Asia and was not improbably more or less akin in signification to the crux ansata of Egypt. The fact that upon very ancient remains still existing the Baal is represented as crowned with a wheel-like nimbus of rays should also be mentioned.

The cross more especially connected with the Phœnician "Bride of the Sun-God" in ancient days, was, as can easily be seen upon reference to ancient coins, where it occurs in the hand of the goddess in question, a long handled cross such as is frequently to be seen in our pictorial representations of John the Baptist.

[1] *Nineveh,* ii. 213.

As John the Baptist was an Asiatic and to some extent a pre-Christian Asiatic, we can here, without wandering very far from the matter in hand, pause to consider the question why we Christians represent John the Baptist, who had nothing to do with a cross, as holding a cross ; if it be not that while Jesus was supposed to represent the Sun in its annual ascension, John was supposed to represent the Sun in its annual declension ? What other rational explanation have we of the facts, (1) that John is represented as saying that he baptised with water but that Jesus would baptise with *fire* (where the rains of winter and the heat of summer may be referred to) ; and (2) that the Christian Church in framing its calendar fixed upon what we call Midsummer day as the birthday of John the Baptist, and upon the day which bears the same relation to the other solstice as the birthday of Christ, as if wishing to illustrate that other remarkable pronouncement of John thus placed at the point where the days begin to shorten, concerning Jesus, thus placed where the days begin to lengthen, " He must increase but I must decrease " ?

The probability that to its, original signification of Life, that of Salvation was added to
the cross as a recognition of the fact that the
salvation of Earth-Life in general and of
Mankind in particular is due to the fact that
at the Vernal Equinox the Sun-God "crosses"
to save, summer and the fruits of the earth
and therefore salvation and increase being due
to the fact that the Sun then crosses the
Equator, is supported by evidence from all
quarters. And if we refuse to admit that
Christianity is permeated with the ideas of
Sun-God worship, we not only have no rational
explanation to offer of the prophecies put by
the Evangelists in the mouth of John the
Baptist to the effect that Jesus would baptise
with *fire* and would *increase*, but also none to
offer of many another prominent feature of
our religion ; such as, for instance, the fact
that while pretending to reverence all the Ten
Commandments we deliberately make a point
of breaking one of them in order to keep as
a day of rest not the seventh day but the
first, the day which from time immemorial was
held sacred throughout the Roman Empire as
Dies Solis, the Day of the Sun. For to aver

as we do that Jesus was not made the subject of a Sun-God allegory, but purposely rose from the underworld on the Day of the Sun, at the time of the Vernal Equinox, in order to annul a commandment previously laid down by God and substitute a new one in silence, is only to make ourselves ridiculous.

Returning however to the matter more particularly in hand, it should be pointed out that the crux ansata mentioned by Layard is not the only kind of cross to be found upon the relics of ancient Babylonia and Assyria. For the cross of four equal arms and the solar wheel are also to be met with.

Moreover, as all visitors to our museums should be aware, the monarchs are represented as wearing in the place of honour round their neck and on their breast, a Maltese cross. And this cross, worn by the kings centuries before our era as the symbol which should above all others be venerated, or as best signifying their power over the lives of their subjects and their position as vice-gerents of the Sun-God, is admitted by all the best authorities to have been the sign and symbol of the Sun-God.[1]

---

[1] *e.g.,* C. W. King, M.A. *Early Christian Numismatics ;* Professor Rawlinson · &c &c.

CHAPTER XVII.

THE PRE-CHRISTIAN CROSS IN AFRICA.

PASSING on to Africa and a consideration of the *crux ansata* or so-called 'Key of the Nile,' we find that this variety of cross had much the same significance attached to it by the ancients as had the more widely accepted varieties.

As a matter of fact no one acquainted with Egyptian antiquities who enquires into the matter in thorough going fashion, can in the end fail to be convinced that the Egyptian cross was a phallic symbol having reference to the sexual powers of generation and to the Sun, and being therefore a symbol both of Life and of the Giver of Life.

The connection between the crux ansata and the Sun-God in the minds of the inhabitants of the Land of the Nile in pre-Christian days, is very clearly set forth by an illustration of Khuenaten in the act of distributing gifts to his courtiers which faces page 40, volume I., of Sir J. Gardner Wilkinson's " *Manners and Customs of the Ancient Egyptians.*" For this monarch—also known as Amenophis IV.—and his wife are both represented as receiving the crux ansata from the Sun-God, and the Sun is marked with the crux ansata as its peculiar symbol.

Upon Plate IV. facing page 43 of the same famous work, we see Seti I. surmounted by the Sun; two crosses adorning the latter. The crosses are, moreover, attached to two serpents issuing from the sun; and these were in ancient days phallic signs representing the sexual powers.

On page 405 is a representation of the Egyptian god Khem, or Amen-Ra Generator · the Egyptian Priapus, or god of Generation. The names of this phallic deity show his connection with the Sun.

It is noteworthy that this particular conception of the Sun-God is accompanied by emblems of the sexual organs of reproduction, and that he bears a St. Andrew's cross upon his breast.

Upon page 24 of volume III. of the same work is another representation of Khem, or Amen-Ra Generator. In this case also he is accompanied by phallic and solar emblems and wears a St. Andrew's cross upon his breast.

On page 26 Sir J. Gardner Wilkinson tells us that

"Khem was considered the generating influence of the sun, whence perhaps the reason of his being connected with Amen-Ra : and in one of the hieroglyphic legends accompanying his name he is styled the sun ; that is the pro-creating power of the only source of warmth, which assists in the continuation of the various created species."

Upon Plate XXII., facing page 44 of volume III., are three different instances of the crux ansata being attached to the sun as the symbol of the Sun-God.

Upon page 46 is another instance of the crux ansata being attached to the solar serpent issuing from the sun's disc.

On Plate XXIII., facing page 52, is another illustration of the reception of the crux ansata from the Sun-God.

Upon page 82 Sir J. Gardner Wilkinson rightly observes that it is absurd to speak of the crux ansata or Egyptian cross as the *Key of the Nile*, inasmuch as this cross "is less frequently seen in the hand of the God Nilus than any deity of the Egyptian pantheon."

Upon the remarkable Plate XXXI., facing page 136, we see inscriptions describing the reigning Pharaoh as the " Vice-gerent of the Giver of Eternal Life "; or, in other words, of the Sun-God. Other expressions applied to the Pharaoh are " Giver of Life and Strength like the Sun "; "Who gives all Life, Stability, and Health like the Sun "; and " Approved of the Sun and Giver of Life like the Sun."

It is thus clear that ages before our era the cross was venerated in Egypt as in other lands as the symbol both of Life and of the Giver of Life ; and that the deity worshipped as the Giver of Life, and ever associated with that salutary symbol the cross, was the Sun-God.

CHAPTER XVIII.

DR. SCHLIEMANN has told us that in his researches upon the site of Troy he found that in pre-Christian if not indeed pre-historic times the cross was, in that classic locality as elsewhere, a phallic emblem and the symbol of life; as well as a solar emblem and the symbol of the holy fire with which life was more or less identified.

For instance on page 337 of his *Ilios* (1880 edition) Dr. Schliemann describes a leaden idol discovered by him and of great antiquity. He tells us that it was female in character and had the vulva marked with the triangle, a symbol of the Feminine Principle. And he points out that within the triangle was the Svastika cross.

On page 521 Dr. Schliemann describes an ancient terra cotta vase, with the characteristics of a woman upon it, and on the vulva a St. Andrew's cross.

Upon page 523 is a reference to another vase of similar design. Here also a cross appears to mark the vulva.

On page 353 Dr. Schliemann admits that the Svastika cross drawn within the triangle marking the vulva, shows that this cross was a sign of generation in ancient and pre-historic times. This remark should evidently have been applied by him to the St. Andrew's cross as well, for he shows that also to have been used as a sign of the organ of generation, as has been shown above.

We are here reminded of the fact, already noted, that the Egyptians represented their God of Generation, Khem, or Amen-Ra Generator, as wearing a conspicuous St. Andrew's cross. And as Khem was the Egyptian Priapus it ought also to be pointed out that it was in ancient times the practice to erect wooden crosses to this conception of the Sun-God.

An illustration of one example of the crosses

erected to Priapus can be seen in figure XI. of plate XXIX. of that well-known work, *Antique Gems and Rings.* [1] And the phallic nature of such crosses cannot be denied.

Returning, however, to the discoveries of Dr. Schliemann upon the site of Troy, we find on page 350 of *Ilios* that both varieties of the Svastika cross are extraordinarily common upon the articles he discovered.

As an Indian symbol the Svastika cross can only be traced back as far as the fourth or fifth century B.C.; and its occurrence upon these and other relics of earlier ages and other lands, shows us that it is inaccurate and misleading to speak of it as " Indian."

The origin of the Svastika cross, whether the 卐 or the 卍, is unknown; but Dr. Schliemann quotes with approval Professor Max Müller's remarks to the effect that Mr. Thomas our distinguished Oriental numismatist

"Has clearly proved that on some of the Andra coins and likewise on some punched coins depicted on Sir W. Elliot's plate IX. *Madras Jour. Lit. and Science,* vol. III., the place of the more definite figure of the

---

[1] C. W. King, M.A.

sun is often taken by the Svastika, and that the Svastika has been inserted within the rings or normal circles representing the four suns of the Ujjain pattern on coins. He has also called attention to the fact that in the long list of the recognised devices of the twenty-four Jaina Tirthankaras the sun is absent; but that while the eighth Tirthankara has the sign of the half-moon the seventh Tirthankara is marked with the *Svastika, i.e.,* the sun. Here then, I think, we have very clear indications that the Svastika, with the hands pointing in the right direction, was originally a symbol of the Sun, perhaps of the vernal sun as opposed to the autumnal sun, the *Sauvastika,* and therefore a natural symbol of light, life, health, and wealth. That in ancient mythology the sun was frequently represented as a wheel is well known. Grimm identifies the Old Norse *hjol* or *hvel,* the A.-S. *hvehol,* English 'wheel,' with κύκλος, Sk. Kakra, wheel; and derives jól, 'yule-tide,' the time of the winter solstice, from hjol, ' the (solar) wheel.' "

Both the 卐 and the 卍 occur upon the famous footprints of Buddha carved upon the Amarâvati Tope, and Dr. Schliemann remarks that we find the Svastika or Sauvastika cross

"In Ezekiel ix. 4, 6, where—in the form of the old Hebrew letter Tau—it is written as the sign of life on the forehead, like the corresponding Indian symbol. We find it twice on a large piece of ornamental leather contained in the celebrated Corneto treasure preserved in the Royal Museum at Berlin; also on ancient pottery found at Konigsberg in the Neumark and preserved in the Märkisches Museum in Berlin ; and on a Bowl from Yucatan in the Berlin Ethnological Museum. We also see it on coins of Gaza, as well as on an Imperial coin of Asido ; also on the drums of the Lapland priests.'

It is noteworthy that in the neighbourhood of Troy, as in Cyprus and other places, a cross of four equal arms, like our sign of addition, in days of old shared with the Svastika crosses the veneration of the people and was evidently more or less akin to those crosses in signification. Dr. Schliemann tells us that this cross of four equal arms " occurs innumerable times on the whorls of the three upper pre-historic cities of Hissarlik," and that if, as Burnouf and others suggest, the 卍 and 卐 represented primitive fire machines, this other cross " might also claim the honour of representing the two pieces of wood for producing the holy fire by friction."

Elsewhere in the same work Dr. Schliemann quotes with approval the opinion of Professor Sayce that the Svastika cross, 卍 or 卐, " was a symbol of generation."

As phallic worship and Sun-God worship were admittedly always closely connected, it is not surprising to find that Dr. Schliemann also very highly commends a dissertation on the 卍 and 卐 by Mr. Edward Thomas, whose conclusion is that

"As far as I have been able to trace or connect the various manifestations of this emblem, they one and all resolve themselves into the primitive conception of solar motion, which was intuitively associated with the rolling or wheel-like projection of the sun through the upper or visible arc of the heavens."

It may therefore be considered proven that the inhabitants of classic Troy like those of the Land of the Nile and other countries, recognised a close affinity between the productive forces and the sun, and were one in accepting a cross of some description as the natural symbol whether of Life or of the Giver of Life.

CHAPTER XIX.

EVIDENCE OF CYPRUS.

ALTHOUGH now, owing to the march of events, the island of Cyprus is out of the way and seldom visited, it was once otherwise. For in days of old it occupied a favoured position between the countries then foremost in the arts of civilisation.

In those days Cyprus was a centre of Phœnician enterprise. And, as we are told in that fine work '*Kypros, the Bible, and Homer : Oriental Civilisation, Art and Religion in ancient times*,' " The oldest extant Phœnician inscriptions, *themselves the earliest examples of letters properly so called*, come from Cyprus."

As, moreover, when face to face with the relics of the Phœnicians we are, as Dr. Max Ohnefalsch Richter also remarks, " In the very midst of

193

ancient Canaanitish civilisation as depicted in the Old Testament," it will be seen that a study of the antiquities of Cyprus should have a special interest for us Christians.

Let us therefore see what the ancient remains found in the island in question, and others referred to in the work mentioned as illustrative of the same, can tell us regarding phallic worship in general and the pre-Christian cross in particular.

One of the first points to be noted in the illustrations supplied by Dr. Max Ohnefalsch-Richter is in a cut of an ancient Cyprian coin on Plate X. ; upon which coin we see over a temple gateway the phallic symbol since adopted by the Moslems, and commonly spoken of as the ' *star* and crescent' although, as already shown, it originally represented the radiate Sun or Male Principle in conjunction with the Crescent moon or Female Principle.

Upon Plate XIX. we see several examples of the Svastika cross occurring upon an ancient Cyprian vase.

On Plate XXV. we are shown a gold leaf taken from an ancient grave, upon which the Svastika cross occurs.

Figure 10 upon the same plate shows us a gold leaf discovered at Amathus upon which we see the Sun and Moon in conjunction, the Sun in this instance being represented as a disc in the horns of the crescent.

Upon Plate XXVI. we have representations of stone pillars at Atheniaon, upon the capitals of which are phallic emblems, including that of the Sun as a disc within the horns of the Crescent moon.

On Plate XXX. we have in figure 7 a cut of an important cylinder now stored in the Berlin Museum, upon which are represented both the Sacred Tree and the Ashera. The winged Sun-disc appears over the former and the Crescent moon over the latter.

Figure 11 upon the same plate shows us a Masseba representing the Male Principle, surmounted by the star-like form which represented the radiate Sun; and an Ashera, representing the Female Principle, surmounted by the Crescent moon.

Just as in modern Christianity we make a distinction without alleging much difference between the Father and the Son, even so in ancient times a distinction of a similarly vague kind was made between the All-Father *Fire* and His Image and First-begotten Son *Light.* The disc of the Sun seems to have represented the former and the Sun-star or radiate Sun the latter where both were represented in one illustration, as for instance in figure 12 on the plate last mentioned.

The illustration in question is an important one. On the left is an Ashera under a Crescent moon ; in the centre is a Masseba under the Sun-star or radiate Sun ; and on the right is an altar under a sun disc.

The phallic meaning of all this is evident ; and a kind of Trinity is presented to us, viz. · (1) The Female Principle and perhaps the primeval Darkness, needing impregnation or illumination ere the same can cause aught to be ; (2) the Male Principle and Light, the First-born Son of Fire ; and (3) Fire itself, the one origin of all things and Father of Spirits, made manifest unto mortals by His First-born Son, and best symbolled, as is Light, by the Solar Orb.

On Plate XXXI. we have in figure 4 a representation of the goddess Ishtar, the bride of the Sun-God. Over her we see the phallic symbol of the radiate Sun and Crescent moon in conjunction.

On Plate XXXII. we see in figure 23 the Svastika cross under a tree, in a representation of a scarab from Ialysos. This cross coupled with the presence of two bulls, one on either side of the tree, seem to show that the Male Principle is referred to.

On Plate XL. we have a cut of a votive arm, holding in its hand that phallic symbol the apple, and obtained from the sanctuary of Apollo at Voni.

On Plate LVIII. in representations of the stone capitals of two votive pillars from the shrine of Aphrodite at Idalion, we see various phallic emblems; including the familiar Sun disc and Crescent moon in conjunction.

The same remark applies to Plate LIX., where two more such pillars are illustrated.

Upon Plate LXIX. are given no less than 134 illustrations of ancient religious symbols, and the phallic character of nearly if not quite all is plainly apparent.

In twelve of these the presence of the Sun or the Crescent Moon as the case may be, points out that in the former event the Male Principle of Life, and in the latter the Female Principle of Life, is referred to. In six other cases the presence of the Sun and Crescent moon in juxtaposition shows that both those Principles are referred to. And in four other examples the presence of the Sun and Crescent moon in conjunction shows that the union of those Principles is referred to.

Besides the numerous Masseboth and Asheroth, respectively representing the Male and Female Principles, we see numerous examples of the triangle which represented the female *vulva* and of the diamond shaped symbol which represented the female *pudendum.*

Among the remaining symbols is the cross of four equal arms.

Upon Plate LXXV. is an illustration of a vase painting in red figures from a Stamnos from Vulci Panofka. The representation is one of the Sun-God Dionysos upon a cross.

The said cross, which like various Christian crosses of the Dark and Middle Ages has projecting branches and foliage, seems to have been more or less connected with the Tree worship of ancient times.

On Plate LXXVI. we are given thirteen

examples of Sacred Trees discovered in the groves of Astarte-Aphrodite and Tanit-Artemis-Cybele, being clay copies of the Sacred Trees erected at the entrances to the temples. As Dr. Ohnefalsch-Richter states, these evidently phallic symbols undoubtedly played a part in the worship of the Sun-God Tammuz-Adonis and his bride Astarte-Aphrodite.

Upon Plate LXXVII. we have a cut of an important Phœnician seal, where we see (1) a man kneeling in adoration to a Divine Trinity connected with the winged disc of the sun, and (2) a priest worshipping three symbols. The three sacred symbols in question are (1) the Ashera or symbol of the Female Life Principle ; (2) the Masseba or symbol of the Male Life Principle ; and (3) a combination of the Ashera and Masseba symbols representing the two Life Principles in conjunction.

On Plate LXXIX. we have in figure 14 a representation both of the Sacred Tree and of the combined Ashera and Masseba. Over the latter we naturally see the radiate Sun and Crescent moon in conjunction.

In figure 16 on the same plate are representations of an Ashera and a Masseba, respectively surmounted by a Crescent moon and a radiate Sun.

A similar remark applies to figure 17. A sacrificing priest can be seen in this and the last named instances.

On Plate LXXX. we have in figure 1 a representation of a holy pillar, the volute capital of which has on it a Crescent moon within the horns of which is a disc plainly marked with a cross. This is taken from an ancient cylinder of Hittite origin.

On the same plate we see in figure 7 a Sun column from Tyre, upon which we see the Crescent and disc in conjunction as in the last case, but without the cross.

On Plate CXVIII. we have in figure 8 a cut of a fine vase from Melos ornamented with a Svastika cross.

Upon Plate CXXXIII. we have, in figures 1 to 4, representations of a sacred Bœotian chest or ark. On the front are seven Svastika crosses (some of each variety) and one ordinary cross like our sign of addition. On the lid we see two serpents surrounded by eight Svastika crosses (some of each variety) and eight crosses formed of tau crosses, ⊞ ; besides two other crosses.

On the back are eight Svastika crosses (some of each variety) and eight other crosses.

In figure 6 we have a cut of a chest from Athiaenon upon which two Svastika crosses will be noticed.

In figure 8 of the same plate is an illustration of one side of another sacred chest or ark from Athiaenon, on which two Svastika crosses of the other variety can be seen.

Upon Plate CLV. we have in figure 9 a cut of an important Cyprian Græco-Phœnician Amphora discovered in an ancient grave at Kition and now stored in the British Museum. The object represented upon it is a Sacred Tree marked at the bottom with a St. Andrew's cross and surrounded with Svastika crosses.

On Plate CLXXIII. we see in group 19 various objects discovered in ancient graves; one bearing several ordinary crosses and also several Svastika crosses, one bearing a Svastika cross of the other variety, and a third bearing Svastika crosses of both kinds.

Upon Plate CXCII. are cuts of various Cyprian coins, the phallic symbol of the circle and cross occurring upon Nos. 1, 9, and 10.

Leaving the Book of Plates and turning to the illustrations given with the Text of the valuable work we are considering, we discover upon page 62 a cut showing the impression of a chalcedony cylinder from the collection of the Duc de Luynes, where the Sun is represented by a Cross of four equal arms.

Upon page 85 we have in figure 117 an illustration of an inscribed cylinder, now belonging to the Bibliothèque Nationale of France, in which, as Dr. Ohnefalsch-Richter remarks, the priest or king represented is raising his arm

"In adoration in the direction of the Cross suspended in the air before him, a holy object we often meet on Assyrian and Babylonian monuments."

This cross, like that last named, is more like a Greek cross than a Maltese cross.

On page 148 we have in figure 150 an illustration of a coloured image of Aphrodite or Astarte discovered in an early Græco-Phœnician tomb at Kurion. This representation of the Goddess of Love and Bride of the Sun-God is marked with several Svastika crosses, and is yet further evidence of the phallic and solar character of that symbol.

Such is the evidence of the phallic worship and Sun-God worship of the Phœnicians and their neighbours, of the close relationship between such phallic worship and Sun-God worship, and of the part played in connection with the same by the pre-Christian cross, borne by a work of research so free from bias against the views of the Christian Church that it has prefixed to it a letter of warm commendation from that veteran statesman and theologian, the author of the ultra-orthodox " *Impregnable Rock of Holy Scripture.*"

CHAPTER XX.

THE most noteworthy features of the available evidence illustrative of the real origin and history of the symbol of the cross have now been placed before the reader, but a number of more or less miscellaneous facts directly or indirectly throwing additional light upon the subject have still to be drawn attention to.

For instance, no mention has yet been made of the *Hermæ* of bygone ages. And although their origin may have had no connection with the symbol in question, it is noteworthy that some at least of the early Christians discovered in the more or less cruciform outline of the Hermæ a reason or excuse for paying them homage, while very similar figures are to be seen illustrated upon Christian antiquities, such as the mosaic of which the great cross of the Lateran forms the principal feature.

The Hermæ venerated by the ancient Greeks were pillars, usually of stone and quadrangular, surmounted in most instances with a head of either Hermes or Dionysos ; and with a peculiar transverse rail just below the head, much used for hanging garlands upon, which made the whole look more or less like a cross.

These pillars were erected in front of temples, tombs, and houses ; but more especially as sign posts at cross roads ; and whether the head at the top was that of Hermes the Messenger of the Gods, or, as was very often the case, that of Dionysos the Sun-God, a phallus was always a prominent feature.

Moreover these phallic and often solar erections called Hermæ, undoubtedly more or less cross-shaped owing to the transverse rail, were worshipped as conducive to fecundity.

It is also worthy of notice that the cross is well known to have been venerated in America before even the Norsemen who preceded Columbus set foot upon that afterwards re-discovered continent.

For instance a cross surrounded by a circle

14

was in use among the ancient Mexicans as a solar sign, another cross was a solar symbol of the natives of Peru from time immemorial, and we are also told by the authorities that a cross of four equal arms with a disc or circle at the centre was the age-old Moqui symbol of the Sun.[1]

Other noteworthy points are that the cross occurs upon Runic monuments in Europe long before Christianity was introduced into the regions containing them ; that ancient altars to the Sun-God Mithras bearing the sacred symbol of the cross have been discovered even in England ; and that the Laplanders of old when sacrificing marked their idols with the symbol of the cross, using the life blood of their victims for that purpose.[2]

It should also be pointed out that on a coin of Thasos bearing representations of a phallic character connected with the worship of the Thracian Bacchus, a Svastika cross is a prominent symbol ; that upon ancient vases the

---

[1] *First Annual Report U.S. Bureau of Ethnology.*
[2] Ol. Varelli, *Scandage Runic ;* Ans. Rudbeckins, *Atlant. :* *e.g.* an altar discovered at Rudchester, Northumberland : Sheffer, *Lapponic.*

headgear of Bacchus is sometimes ornamented with the cross of four equal arms; that upon a Greek vase at Lentini, Sicily, an ancient representation of the Sun-God Hercules is accompanied by no less than three different kinds of crosses as symbols ; and that upon an archaic Greek vase in the British Museum, the Svastika cross, the St. Andrew's cross, and the other and right angled cross of four equal arms, appear under the rays of the Sun. Nor should it be forgotten that though the Svastika cross has almost died out as a Christian symbol and was perhaps never thoroughly acclimatised as such, it often appeared upon Christian ecclesias tical properties of the Middle Ages, and, either as a Pagan or Christian symbol, continually occurs in the catacombs of Rome.

We are told that circular wafers or cakes were used in the mysteries of the Sun-God Bacchus, and, being marked with a cross, resembled the disc-like wafers of the Christian Mass. Whether this was so or not, it is note-worthy that a cross is said to appear upon the representation of a circular wafer used in the mysteries of Mithras which occurs upon an ancient fresco at Rome.

14a

In this connection it may be mentioned, as a series of curious coincidences, that in the Zoroastrian religion long before our era the Sun-God Mithras bore much the same relation to the All-Father that the Christ does in ours, and is referred to in the Zend Avesta as the *Incarnate Word;* that Mithras is said, like the Christ, to have been born in a cave; that the Fathers admitted that the new-born Sun had been worshipped in the cave at Bethlehem to which the story of the birth of Jesus referred; and that in framing its calendar our Church fixed upon the recognised birthday of Mithras, the *Natalis Invicti* of the Roman Brumalia, as the birthday of the Christ.

It is also noteworthy that the Christ is thus said to have been born as well as to have risen again the third *or fourth* ("*After* three days," *Matt.* xxvii. 63; *after* "Three days and three nights," Matt. xii. 40) day. For the birthday of Mithras and afterwards of the Christ, known to us as Christmas day, seems to have been fixed upon as the third or fourth day after the winter solstice, and as that upon which the sun's resurrection from the south was first discernible after its apparent cessation of movement or death.

In this connection it should be added that Lucian records the fact that the Sun-God referred to by the Fathers as worshipped at Bethlehem was lamented as dead once a year and always acclaimed as alive again the third day ; that in several places in the Zend Avesta we meet with passages which show that the Mithras worshippers of old believed that at the death of a man his spirit sits at the head of the corpse for three days and three nights, and then, at dawn, rises free from all earthly attachments ; and that we say that the execution of Jesus took place at the time of the Passover or Vernal Equinox, while instead of the prophesied " three days and three nights in the heart of the earth " (*Matt.* xii. 40) the period between the death and burial on Good Friday evening and the resurrection before dawn on Easter Sunday is just about that during which the Sun's disc is at the Vernal Equinox transfixed by the Equator, *viz.*, $32\frac{2}{3}$ hours.

The question why the Cock so often, like the Cross, surmounts the steeples wherewith we adorn our Christian churches, is brought before us by the fact that it was in ancient days a well-known symbol both of the generative

powers and of the Sun-God ; often appearing
as such upon the top of a sacred pillar in
Assyrian and Babylonian representations of
priests in the act of sacrificing or worshipping.
It was probably as the " herald of the dawn "
that this bird became a symbol of the Sun
God, and it would seem that we place its
effigy aloft with the same idea in view.

Another point to be noted is that in the
Kunthistorisches Museum at Vienna is an
ancient vase upon which is a representation of
the Sun-God Apollo bearing upon his breast
as his one ornament and symbol a Svastika
cross.

We are reminded of the facts that we
Christians were once in the habit of alluding
to the cross as the Tree of Life, and that
the ancients dressed up the trunks of trees
and worshipped them as symbols of life and
growth, by an Attic vase of the fifth century
B.C.   Upon this is a red coloured painting of
a tree so dressed, on which is to be seen
n ear the top a head of the Sun-God Dionysos,
and surrounding the trunk a shirt or garment
covered with crosses.

As to the evidence obtained from the ruins

of Herculaneum and Pompeii, it is said that much which is of a phallic character has been, from quite worthy motives, kept in the background. An important fact has however been mentioned by Mr. C. W. King, M.A., in his well known work on the *Gnostics and their Remains*, and this at least can be commented upon. He tells us that the Cross and the Phallus were found placed in juxtaposition upon the walls as meaning one and the same thing, and he goes on to add that

"This cross seems to be the Egyptian Tau, that ancient symbol of the generative power and therefore transferred into the Bacchic mysteries."

The foregoing are the last of the evidences throwing light upon the origin and history of the symbol adopted by our religion as its own, which the author thinks it necessary to bring forward in support of his contention. And however much of the evidence sought out by the author and in this work marshalled by him into something like order may seem by itself to be untrustworthy or worthless, no reader can reasonably deny that it has been proved that the cross was a well known symbol of Life long before our era, and that as a whole the evidence tends to show that it became such as a phallic symbol, and therefore as a symbol of the Sun-God.

And what is the moral of the real, as distinguished from the imaginary, history of the symbol of the cross but this : that from the beginning nought has caused the beliefs of men to assume an appearance of radical difference, save the difference in the name or dress with which this or that set of men have clothed similar ideas?

For, as has already been hinted, Humanity has ever had but one God and but one Religion. And as from one point of view Life is but another term for the Real Presence, and Death but another term for the withdrawal of Deity, it may be said that that God is Life, and that Religion the desire for Life, more Life, and fuller Life. Moreover, as has been said before, this universal worship of Life is discernible even in the willingness of some to sacrifice what remains to them of mortal life in the hope of thus being enabled to lay hold of a life immortal which is not for all.

The worship of Life is natural, and must of necessity continue. Let us however render it nobler by recognising its catholicity; and by contemptuously refusing to either seek or accept a life of bliss hereafter which any of our brothers and sisters are, either in our imagination or in reality, to be debarred from sharing.

CHAPTER XXI.

SUMMARY.

A T the commencement of this work it was shown that, as the Greek text of the writings forming the New Testament testifies, not one of the Apostles or Evangelists ever stated that Jesus was executed upon a cross-shaped instrument of execution. The circumstances under which the figure of the cross became the symbol of our religion, were then made clear. And, having since demonstrated the existence in pre-Christian ages of a wide-spread veneration of the figure of the cross as the symbol of Life and of the Sun-God, which may have given rise to the desire to associate Jesus therewith, little remains for the author to do save draw the notice of the reader to the admissions of other writers concerning the rise of the cross as the symbol of Christianity ; for the sake of brevity more or less confining his attention to two well known works upon the history of religious art.

It should first however be pointed out that though we Christians affirm that crucifixion was a form of capital punishment made use of in days of old, and abolished the fourth century after Christ by Constantine because Jesus was so executed, we cannot exactly prove that the *staurosis* thus abolished was crucifixion, or even that it included crucifixion. For various as are the different forms of ' death by the stauros' of which descriptions have come down to us from pre-Christian ages and the first three centuries of our era, no relic of that date bears a representation of an instrument of execution such as we cause to appear in our sacred pictures, and even if, regardless of the more exact meaning of the word stauros, we suppose the term staurosis to have included every form of carrying out the extreme penalty by means of affixion or suspension, we meet with no description of such an instrument of execution as we picture.

Therefore even if we were to exclude from the staurosis abolished by Constantine all forms of transfixion by a stauros, we could not, upon the evidence before us, fairly say that what that astute Emperor abolished was what is usually understood by the term crucifixion.

It will not be necessary to quote again the admission of the Reverend S. Baring-Gould, M.A., to the effect that the so-called Cross of Constantine or monogram of Christ was but the symbol of the Sun-God of the Gauls with a loop added by their crafty leader to please the Christians, but it may be pointed out that this fact is also admitted in *Chambers's Encyclopædia;* where we read that

"The so-called cross of Constantine was not really a cross but a circle containing the X P I, the first three letters of the name of Christ in Greek ; and was merely an adaptation of a symbol of a Gaulish solar deity."

And it may be added that the fact that the Monogram of Christ and the ordinary cross so frequently used as symbols by Constantine upon his coins and elsewhere, and thus made symbols of the Roman Empire in the first half of the fourth century, were at first Pagan rather than Christian symbols, also seems to be borne out by Dean Burgon in his *Letters from Rome,* where he states

"I question whether a cross occurs on any Christian monument of the first four centuries" [1]

Passing on however to the representative works on Christian Art already referred to, we first come to Mrs. Jameson's famous *History of Our Lord as exemplified in works of art.*

Upon page 315 of Volume II. the gifted authoress, after confessing that the cross was venerated by the heathen as a symbol of Life before the period of Christianity and referring to St. Chrysostom, who flourished half a century after Constantine, admits that

"It must be owned that ancient objects of Art, as far as hitherto known, afford no corroboration of the use of the cross in the simple transverse form familiar to us at any period preceding or even closely succeeding the words of St. Chrysostom."

That is to say, although Constantine introduced the Monogram of Christ and the cross of four equal arms before St. Chrysostom was born, and, making them symbols of the Roman

[1] *Letters from Rome,* 1862, p. 210.

Empire, would, whether a Sun-God worshipper or a Christian, in any case have imposed them upon what he established as his State Religion, it was not till after these solar symbols of the Gauls were accepted as Christian that such a cross as could possibly have been a representation of an instrument of execution was introduced.

As to the crucifix, we are told that though this is said by some to be referred to in the works of St. Gregory of Nyssa—a Bishop of Tours who lived in the sixth century, and also in the injunctions of the often quoted council of Greek bishops A.C. 692 called the "Quini-sextum" or "in Trullo," the evidence is

"Insufficient to convince most modern archæologists that a crucifix in any sense now accepted was meant."

In other words, not only is it clear that the cross as a representation of the instrument of execution upon which Jesus died was not introduced till after the days of Constantine, but it is also evident that the crucifix, the earliest known representation of that execution, was not introduced till centuries later.

Other noteworthy admissions are made in the work above quoted from, but we must pass on to the Dean of Canterbury's comparatively recent work upon the same subject.

Dean Farrar states upon page 11 of his *Life of Christ as represented in Art* that

"Of all early Christian symbols the *Fish* was the most frequent and the favourite."

The Fish; and not the Cross.

Moreover the Dean significantly adds upon the next page, that the Fish

"Continued to be a common symbol down to the days of Constantine."

And the significance lies in the fact that the introduction by Constantine of the solar symbols venerated by the Gauls, may account for the displacement of the symbol of the Fish from favour.

Upon page 19 Dr. Farrar goes on to say that

"Two symbols continued for ages to be especially common, of which I have not yet spoken. They were not generally adopted, even if they appeared at all, until after the Peace of the Church at the beginning of the fourth century. I mean the cross and the monogram of Christ."

Here again, it will be seen, the Dean admits that the cross, as the symbol of our religion, came in with Constantine.

Directly after the passage last quoted Dean Farrar very misleadingly remarks : " It must be remembered that the cross was in itself an object of utter horror even to the Pagans." For the exact reverse is the truth, inasmuch as in almost every land a cross of some description had been for ages venerated as a symbol of Life.

The fact of course is that the Dean here and elsewhere, like other Christian writers, does not take the trouble to distinguish between the symbol of the cross and the death caused by execution upon a stauros ; which instrument, by the way, was, as has been shown, not necessarily in the shape of a cross, and appears to have been in most cases a stake without a transverse rail. What the Pagans held in utter horror was the awful death caused by trans-fixion by or affixion to a stauros, whatever its shape ; the symbol of the cross was, upon the contrary, an object of veneration among them from time immemorial.

On page 23 Dr. Farrar, alluding to the use

of the transient sign of the cross by the Christians of early days, makes the admission

"That it did *not* remind them of the Crucifixion only or even mainly is proved alike by their literature and other relics."

Exactly so: for the non-material sign traced by them (and by us) upon the forehead in the *non-Mosaic* initiatory rite of baptism and perhaps also upon the breast or in the air at other times, seems to have been the survival of a Pagan and pre-Christian custom.

Upon page 24 Dean Farrár admits that

"The cross was only introduced among the Christian symbols tentatively and timidly. It may be doubted whether it once occurs till after the vision of Constantine in 312 and his accession to the Empire of the East and West in 324."

Further on upon the same page the Dean of Canterbury, passing without notice from symbols to instruments of execution and making no distinction whatever, states that

"Crosses were of two kinds. The *Crux Simplex*, 'of one single piece without transom,' was a mere stake, used sometimes to impale, sometimes to hang the victim by the hands."

Exactly so.

But, to bring this work to a conclusion with what is the crux of the whole matter, is it not disingenuous in the extreme upon the part of those of us Christians who know better, to hide the fact that it may have been upon some such cross as the Dean here refers to, that is, upon no cross at all, that Jesus was executed? Is it not dishonest of us to place before the masses Bibles and Lexicons wherein we ever carefully translate as "cross" a word which at the time the ancient classics and our sacred writings were penned did not necessarily, if indeed ever, signify something cross-shaped? Is it not gross disloyalty to Truth to insist, as we do in our versions of the Christian Scriptures, upon translating as "crucify" or "crucified" four different words, not one of which referred to anything necessarily in the shape of a cross?

Another point which should be mentioned though such matters cannot be discussed here, is that the questions whether Jesus did not prophesy that the final Day of Judgment would come before those whom he addressed should die, and did not solemnly declare that his mission was to the descendants of Jacob or Israel and to them alone, undoubtedly affect our story.

As to the Gospel of the Cross, have not we Christians by, in our imaginations, limiting its saving effects to the few who are able to believe in it, all the centuries that we have re-echoed the cry " the Kingdom of Heaven is at hand " *forced* upon the same the unutterably selfish meaning that the kingdom at hand for the many who simply cannot believe is that of Hell? Was *that* what Jesus meant, and all that the so-called cross effected?

Moreover, whether the message of Jesus which we proclaim and variously interpret was or was not a gospel—that is, " glad tidings "—to all men, and from an unselfish point of view, what possible good purpose can be served by insisting upon supplementing the simple story of his stressful life, his magnificent love for the afflicted and suffering, his equally magnificent hatred of qualities not altogether dissimilar from that which enables some of us to claim to be not only admirers but also genuine followers of a Communist who declared that those who would follow him must first sell all their possessions and give the proceeds to the poor;—what good purpose can be served by supplementing this, and the account of the final conflict of Jesus with the officials of his native land and his subsequent execution upon a **stauros** or stake not stated to have had a cross-bar attached, by the adoption and culture of a partisan and misleading fiction regarding the origin and history of the symbol of the cross ?

THE END.

.

Made in the USA
Las Vegas, NV
27 February 2024

86345999R00125